Key Stage 3

MATHS

Homework Book

Author - Richard English
Series Editor - Alwyn Morgan

Acknowledgements

This publication is dedicated to all parents who try to help their children with their homework, and all of those who might not necessarily seek to help, but still care dearly about their children's education.

I would also like to express my sincere thanks to the authors for responding so well to the challenge of producing these materials, and Letts Educational for their vision and commitment in promoting the role of parents in their children's education.

Finally, I would like to thank my wife, Carole, for her support, encouragement and patience.

Alwyn Morgan

First published 1998

Letts Educational, Schools and Colleges Division, 9-15 Aldine Street, London W12 8AW
Tel: 0181 740 2270, Fax: 0181 740 2280

Design by Tessa Barwick and Dave Glover

Project Management Rosine Faucompré

British Library Cataloguing-in-Publication Data

A CIP record for this book is available from the British Library

ISBN 1 84085 0159

Printed in Great Britain by Bath Press Ltd

Letts Educational is the trading name of BPP (Letts Educational) Ltd

CONTENTS

An Introduction for Parents and Pupils

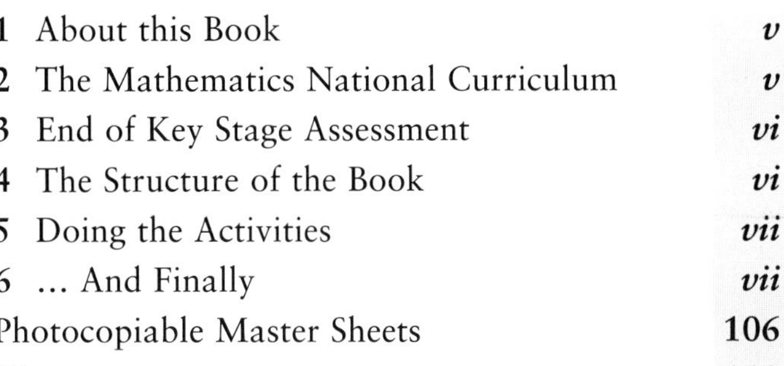

AN INTRODUCTION FOR PARENTS AND PUPILS

1 ~ About this Book

This book provides 100 mathematical activities to be completed at home but they are much more than just 'homework'. The key feature is that every activity requires the pupil to work with a parent or other adult in the family. This way of working offers many benefits for both the pupil and the parent:

- Mathematics is not something which takes place only in the classroom. Young children start school with a wealth of knowledge based on their everyday experiences at home and they continue to learn in this way throughout their lives. Education should therefore be seen as a partnership between the school and the home.

- Parents want to be involved in their children's education. They want to know about the work that is being covered and about how well their child is doing. What better way is there for these wishes to be fulfilled than for parents to actually do mathematics with their children at home?

- Mathematics should not be carried out in silence on your own. We learn mathematics by discussing, exploring, discovering, explaining and working with other people. In this way parents and children can learn mathematics together at home.

- Many adults have a negative attitude towards mathematics and openly admit to being weak in this area. The activities in this book show that it is possible for everyone to experience success in mathematics and that it is something to be enjoyed rather than feared.

2 ~ The Mathematics National Curriculum

Key Stage 3 refers to the first three years of secondary school (Year 7, Year 8 and Year 9). The Key Stage 3 Programme of Study sets out the mathematics that pupils should be taught during these three years. The mathematics is divided into five broad areas:

Using and Applying Mathematics is all about using and applying the knowledge, skills and understanding specified in the other four sections. It is concerned with things such as making decisions, communicating mathematics and working logically to solve problems.

Number includes work on the number system, calculations and solving number problems.

Algebra is all about patterns and relationships; spotting patterns, continuing patterns, predicting patterns and being able to make and use rules which produce patterns.

Shape, Space and Measures looks at the properties of two- and three-dimensional shapes and the ways that we can move these shapes around. It also includes work on measuring time, distance, speed, area, volume, capacity and mass.

Handling Data involves collecting, representing, analysing and interpreting various types of information. It also includes work on probability.

The activities in this book cover all of these areas of mathematics and cater for a wide range of mathematical ability. Each activity indicates the sections of the Programme of Study that are being covered.

3 ~ End of Key Stage Assessment

At the end of Key Stage 3 pupils' mathematical ability is assessed in two ways: by written national tests and by teacher assessment. Both of these are reported to parents in terms of a level. By the end of Key Stage 3 pupils should be working somewhere in the range of level 3 to level 8. The higher the level the better the performance. An average pupil at the end of Key Stage 3 is expected to achieve level 5 or 6.

4 ~ The Structure of the Book

The activities are broadly arranged according to the areas of mathematics identified above. The Number activities appear first, followed by Shape, Space and Measures activities, then Algebra activities, and finally Handling Data activities. Using and Applying Mathematics permeates all of the activities. Many of them touch upon several different areas of mathematics and so it is not obvious where they should appear in the order.

The activities are not arranged in order of difficulty and it is not intended that you work through every page starting with the first. It is therefore likely that the teacher will 'dip in' to the book and select activities which are suitable for the age and ability of the class and fit in with the mathematics being taught at the time.

Each activity is divided into a number of sections.

Aim indicates what you should achieve by completing the activity.

National Curriculum lists the relevant sections from the Programme of Study.

Background provides a brief introduction to the activity.

Homework Activity describes what must be done.

Ask the Family is the part which requires collaboration with other people at home. Sometimes this is a separate section, sometimes the whole activity must be done with someone at home.

5 ~ Doing the Activities

Every activity involves writing, drawing or recording of some sort, and it is important that this is done clearly and carefully because the teacher will probably want to mark the work or use it as the basis of further activities at school.

None of the activities require any special equipment or apparatus. Most can be completed using a basic maths 'toolkit' comprising

a pen

a pencil

a ruler

paper

a calculator

Occasionally you will need a dice, a couple of counters, coins, scissors and glue or sticky tape. Some activities require graph paper, spotty paper or some other special sheet. These will be provided by the teacher when necessary.

6 ~ ... And Finally

The whole purpose of putting together the activities in this book was to allow pupils and their families to learn maths together in an enjoyable way so as to remove some of the fear and mystery that surrounds the subject. I hope the activities are both stimulating and enjoyable and make you want to learn, use and explore mathematics for many years to come.

Richard English

April 1998

PLAY YOUR CROWDS RIGHT

Aims:

~To practise estimating skills in a real-life situation~

~To give reasons for your estimates~

National Curriculum:

~Using and Applying Mathematics 1a, 4a; Number 3f, 4c~

Background:

~This activity provides valuable estimating practice. It is important to realise that we don't always have to get something exactly right. Sometimes a rough answer or ***estimate*** *is good enough.~*

Homework Activity – Ask the Family

Get a list of next Saturday's Premier League football fixtures.

- Number the matches 1, 2, 3 ... until each match is numbered.
- For each odd-numbered match estimate what the size of the crowd will be.
- For each even-numbered match get someone at home to estimate the size of the crowd.
- For each even-numbered match decide whether you think the crowd will be bigger or smaller than the estimate the other person has made.
- Similarly the other person must decide whether the odd-numbered matches will be bigger or smaller than your estimate.
- You could record all of the information in a table like this.

	FIXTURE	CROWD ESTIMATE	BIGGER OR SMALLER?	ACTUAL CROWD	WHO WAS NEARER?
1	Arsenal v Liverpool	34,500	smaller		
2	Aston Villa v Man. Utd.	44,650	bigger		

- After the matches have been played, find out what the attendances were and write them on the table. Then you can see who was right.
- Discuss the things you need to think about when deciding what the size of the crowd will be. Why do some matches have very large crowds and others have much smaller crowds?
- Make a list of the reasons for the differences.

PLAY YOUR CROWDS RIGHT AGAIN

Homework Activity – Ask the Family

Get a list of next Saturday's Premier League football fixtures. For each match estimate what the size of the crowd will be.

You could record the information in the first two columns of a table like this.

FIXTURE	CROWD ESTIMATE	ACTUAL CROWD	ERROR
Everton v Chelsea	29,000		
Spurs v Leeds Utd.	36,750		

- Ask someone at home to do the same for the matches in Division Three. Make sure they have to make the same number of estimates as you do, for example eight matches in the Premier League for you and the first eight matches in Division Three for them.
- After the matches have been played, find out the actual attendances and fill in the 3rd and 4th columns of the two tables.
- Work out your total error and ask the other person to work out theirs.
- Who has the lowest total error?
- Is the person with the lowest total error the best at estimating football crowds?
- Is the total error the best way of judging how good you are at estimating?
- Give reasons for your answer.
- Can you think of a better way of deciding who is better at estimating?
- Who is better at estimating using the new method?
- Explain why the new method is better.

Aims:

~To practise estimating skills in a real-life situation~

~To look at ways of comparing how good different estimates are~

National Curriculum:

~Using and Applying Mathematics 1a, 2a, 2b, 4a; Number 2b, 3d, 3f, 4a, 4b~

Background:

~This is an extension of the earlier activity ***Play Your Crowds Right*** *on page 2 and so provides more valuable practice at estimating. This time you have to think carefully about ways of judging how good an estimate is. Does it matter if we are 3 metres out when we estimate a distance? Was it a good estimate or not? How can we tell?~*

THE PRICE IS RIGHT

Aims:

~*To practise and develop your mental arithmetic skills in the context of money*~

~*To explain and discuss various ways of doing mental calculations*~

National Curriculum:

~*Using and Applying Mathematics 2a, 2b; Number 1b, 3b*~

Background:

~*We all need to have good mental arithmetic skills but it is also important to realise that there are often several different ways of doing the same calculation. This activity looks at both of these key issues.*~

Homework Activity

1 Look at the prices of socks and shirts above. In your head work out the cost of:

- four pairs of socks.
- ten pairs of socks.
- five shirts.
- twelve shirts.

Write down your answers.

2 In your own words, describe how you worked out each answer.

3 Why do you think a lot of prices end with 95p or 99p? Write down your reasons.

~ Ask the family ~

Discuss with someone at home the reasons why a lot of prices end with 95p or 99p.

Explain to someone at home the ways that you worked out the answers in part 1.

Get them to explain how they would have done it.

Are their methods the same as yours?

If they are different then write down a brief explanation of their methods.

EGYPTIAN MULTIPLICATION

Homework Activity

Try to follow this way of working out 18 x 53.

Write 1 at the left and the bigger number on the right.

Work down, doubling the numbers each time.

Stop when the number on the left is more than half of the smaller number in the original multiplication.

1	53
2	106
4	212
8	424
16	848

Look for numbers on the left which add up to 18 (16 and 2).

Cross out all of the other rows of numbers.

Add up the remaining numbers on the right.

(106 + 848 = 954)

~~1~~	~~53~~
2	106
~~4~~	~~212~~
~~8~~	~~424~~
16	848
	954

Use Egyptian multiplication to work out:

(a) 45 x 28 (b) 36 x 47 (c) 27 x 34

(d) 73 x 39 (e) 29 x 113

Check your answers with a calculator.

~ Ask the family ~

Make up five multiplications like the ones above.

Have a competition with someone at home.

You use Egyptian multiplication and they can use whatever method they want (but no calculators). See who can do the five multiplications the quickest (and get the answers right!).

Explain Egyptian multiplication to them.

Aims:

~ To explore alternative methods of doing pencil and paper arithmetic~

~ To practise one of these methods~

National Curriculum:

~ Using and Applying Mathematics 1a; Number 1b, 3a, 3b~

Background:

~ Do you have problems with pencil and paper long multiplication? Here is an alternative method based on doubling and addition which was used by the Ancient Egyptians.~

RUSSIAN MULTIPLICATION

Aims:

~To explore alternative methods of doing pencil and paper arithmetic~

~To practise one of these methods~

National Curriculum:

~Using and Applying Mathematics 1a; Number 1b, 3a, 3b~

Background:

~This method of multiplication was used by Russians many years ago and is based on halving, doubling and addition. Give it a try and see how it compares with other methods you know.~

Homework Activity

Try to follow this way of working out 42 x 33.

12	33
21	66
10	132
5	264
2	528
1	1056

Halve the number on the left, ignoring any halves.

Double the number on the right.

Stop when the number on the left is 1.

Cross out all the rows where the number on the left is even.

Add up the remaining numbers on the right.

(66 + 264 + 1056 = 1386)

~~42~~	~~33~~
21	66
~~10~~	~~132~~
5	264
~~2~~	~~528~~
1	1056
	1386

Use Russian multiplication to work out:

(a) 17 x 24 (b) 36 x 19 (c) 27 x 31

(d) 51 x 23 (e) 39 x 112

Check your answers with a calculator.

~ Ask the family ~

Make up five multiplications like the ones above.

Have a competition with someone at home.

You use Russian multiplication and they can use whatever method they want (but no calculators). See who can do the five multiplications the quickest (and get the answers right!).

Explain Russian multiplication to them.

ROUND 'EM UP (OR ROUND 'EM DOWN)?

Homework Activity

Use a Sunday newspaper to find out the attendance figures for:

- five Premier League matches
- five Division One matches
- five Division Two matches.

Write down the exact attendance figures and then round them as described below.

- Round the Premier League figures to the nearest 10000.
- Round the Division One figures to the nearest 1000.
- Round the Division Two figures to the nearest 100.

~ Ask the family ~

Show someone at home what you have been doing and explain to them how you rounded the figures.

Together, find several examples of figures that are not exact. Good places to look are newspapers, encyclopaedias and atlases.

Talk about the examples you have found.

You might like to discuss questions such as:

- How do you know the figures are not exact?
- How rough are they?
- Why have exact figures not been used?
- When is it sensible to round to the nearest million?
- When is it sensible to round to the nearest ten?

Aims:

~ To round numbers to the nearest 10000, 1000 and 100~

~ To understand the reasons why we use rough figures~

National Curriculum:

~ Using and Applying Mathematics 3a; Number 2a, 3f~

Background:

*~ We are told that the distance to the Sun is 93 million miles and the population of Great Britain is 50 million but are these the true figures? If not, why do we use them? This activity provides practice at using **approximate** figures and also looks at the reasons why we use them.~*

ROUNDING WITH A CALCULATOR

Aim:

~To round numbers to the nearest whole number~

National Curriculum:

~Using and Applying Mathematics 3a; Number 1a, 2a, 3e, 3f;~

Background:

~When we measure distances, times, weights, areas and volumes, or when we work out the answer to a calculation, we don't always have to be exact. Sometimes an ***approximate*** *answer is good enough. This activity provides practice at rounding exact answers to the nearest whole number.~*

Homework Activity

Pick any number from list A.

Pick any number from list B.

Use a calculator to divide the list A number by the list B number.

Make sure you write down the numbers you use and the exact answer shown on the calculator.

Round the exact answer to the nearest whole number and write it down.

Repeat this until you have done 12 calculations altogether.

LIST A	400	750	120	360	950	80
LIST B	23	185	42	65	88	140

~ Ask the family ~

Talk to someone at home about rounding. Explain to them how you have rounded your answers to the nearest whole number.

Talk about the answers to these two questions.

1 Is 7.5 cm nearer to 7 cm or nearer to 8 cm?

2 What is 7.5 cm rounded to the nearest centimetre?

Try to think of a few everyday examples of how we use approximate figures or quantities instead of exact ones. Write down the examples you think of.

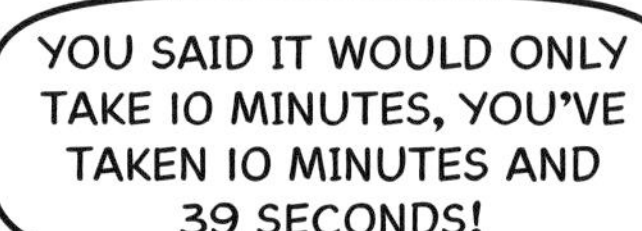

MORE ROUNDING WITH A CALCULATOR

Homework Activity – Ask the Family

Write down all the prime numbers between 10 and 100. (A prime number is only divisible by itself and 1.)

Write each number on a small piece of paper.

Put all the pieces of paper in a container.

Pick two numbers without looking.

Use a calculator to divide the first number by the second number.

Write down the two numbers and the answer shown on the calculator.

Put the two numbers back in the container and keep repeating this process until you have done 12 calculations altogether.

Now you must round the 12 exact answers you have written down.

- Round the first four answers to one decimal place.
- Round the next four answers to two decimal places.
- Round the last four answers to three decimal places.

Make sure you write down your rounded answers and explain to the other person how you are doing it – they might not know how to round numbers to decimal places.

Aims:

~To identify prime numbers~

~To round numbers to a certain number of decimal places~

National Curriculum:

~Using and Applying Mathematics 3a; Number 1a, 2a, 3a, 3e, 3f~

Background:

*~In order to work out a rough answer to a complex calculation we need to be able to round the numbers to one, two or three decimal places. This activity provides important practice at **approximating** and can be done with the help of someone at home.~*

MONEY TROUBLE

Aims:

~To use a calculator to solve everyday problems involving money~

~ To interpret the answers provided by a calculator~

National Curriculum:

~Using and Applying Mathematics 1a; Number 1a, 1b, 2a, 3e, 4b, 4d~

Background:

~Some everyday money situations involve fractions of a penny. An electronic calculator can deal with these amounts easily but we need to know the real meaning of the answers the calculator provides for us.~

Homework Activity

You can use a calculator to help you answer these questions but your work should be clear and make sense to anyone reading it.

1 If you share £100 equally between seven people, how much would each person get?

2 Share £100 between seven people again, but this time the money consists of only notes and £1 coins (there is no small change).

3 Petrol costs 65.9 pence per litre. How much (in pounds and pence) will 32 litres cost?

4 Someone travelling to the United States can get 1.647 US dollars for each £1. How many dollars and cents will they get for £225?

5 A cheap-rate telephone call to the United States costs 24.5 pence per minute.

- How much does it cost per second?
- How much (in pounds and pence) will it cost for a call lasting 4 minutes 26 seconds?

~ Ask the family ~

Show these questions to someone at home and explain how you worked out the answers. Together, think of other examples of everyday money situations which involve fractions of a penny. Make a note of the examples you think of.

MULTIPLICATION RACE

Homework Activity – Ask the Family

59 71 12 18 26 40 22 23 6 30 37 13 15 7 4

INSTRUCTIONS

Player One places a counter on the 7 stepping stone.
Player Two places a counter on the 4 stepping stone.
Take it in turns to have a go.
Estimate the number you need to multiply by to get to the next stepping stone.
Check with a calculator (round answer to nearest whole number).
If you are right you can move to the next stone.
The winner is the first to visit all of the stepping stones.

EXAMPLE:

Player One is on 7 and wants to get to 13.
He tells Player Two that the multiplier is 1.7.
Player Two checks with a calculator.

7 x 1.7 = 11.9

(12 to the nearest whole number)

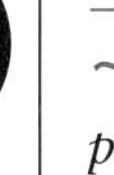

Player One cannot move to the next stone.
He can try again next time (perhaps he'll try 1.8)
Player Two is on 4 and wants to get to 15.
She says the multiplier is 3.7.
Player One checks with a calculator.

4 x 3.7 = 14.8

(15 to the nearest whole number)

Player Two moves to the next stone.
Then it's Player One's turn again.

Aims:

~To estimate and approximate using decimals~

~To use trial and improvement methods (trial and error)~

National Curriculum:

~Using and Applying Mathematics 1a, 2a; Number 1a, 1b, 2a, 3c, 3f, 4b~

Background:

~This game, for two players, provides valuable practice at estimating and approximating in relation to decimals multiplication. If you find it difficult to play using this book, you could make a quick copy of the number track on a large piece of paper.~

G'ZINTA

Aims:

~To find ways of checking for divisibility~

~To solve problems involving division~

National Curriculum:

~Using and Applying Mathematics 1a, 2a, 2b, 3a; Number 2a, 3a~

Background:

~These activities are all about g'zintas ("It's a g'zinta!" = goes into = division. Get it?).~

Homework Activity

1 How can you tell that a number is divisible by 10 just by looking at it? How can you tell that a number is divisible by 5?

2 Do you know any quick ways of checking for divisibility by any other numbers? Ask people at home if they know. Write down all of the ones that you know or find out about.

3 The smallest number which is divisible by 2, 3, 4 and 5 is 60. Find the smallest number which is divisible by:

- All the numbers from 1 to 10.
- All the odd numbers up to 9.
- All the even numbers up to 10.
- All the numbers from 1 to 20.

You can use a calculator if you want to. In your own words, briefly explain how you found each answer.

G'ZINTA!

~ Ask the family ~

Try this division trick with people at home.
Ask them to write down any 3-figure number and then repeat it to form a 6-figure number, for example 207207.
Ask them to divide the 6-figure number by 7.
Impress them by saying "ignore any remainder or decimals because there won't be any".
Ask them to divide the answer by 11.
Again tell them there won't be any remainder or decimals.
Ask them to divide the answer by 13.
The answer should be their original 3-figure number.

How does the trick work? (Hint: Try multiplying 7, 11 and 13.)

AGAINST THE CLOCK

Homework Activity – Ask the Family

Write each of the digits 0 to 9 on a separate piece of card.

Each player will need a pen and a piece of paper to write on.

You will also need a clock or watch.

Agree on a target number before each round of the game.

Place the ten cards face down on the table.

Pick four cards, but keep them face down until everyone is ready.

When the cards are turned over everyone has a set amount of time (e.g. 30 seconds or 1 minute) to use the four digits to make the target number.

All four digits must be used once and only once.

You must not use a calculator.

When the time is up call out "stop" and everyone should put their pens down.

Check the expressions with a calculator if necessary.

If you make the target number, score 5 points.

If you are no more than 5 from the target number, score 2 points.

If you are no more than 10 from the target number, score 1 point.

EXAMPLE:

Suppose the target is 150 and cards 1, 2, 5 and 9 are turned over.

PLAYER ONE	92 + 51 = 143	SCORE 1 POINT
PLAYER TWO	(29 + 1) X 5 = 150	SCORE 5 POINTS
PLAYER THREE	(9 + 5) X 12 = 168	SCORE 0 POINTS

Aims:

~To practise a wide range of arithmetic skills~

~To use numbers and symbols in the right order~

National Curriculum:

~Using and Applying Mathematics 1a, 1b, 2a, 3a; Number 1b, 2a, 3b, 4a, 4b~

Background:

~This game for two or more people provides valuable practice at arithmetic skills and should be good fun at the same time.~

NAME THE DAY

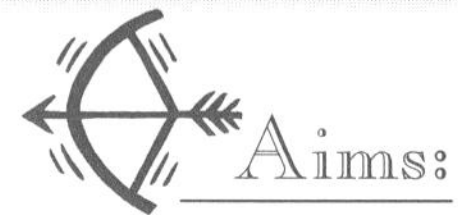

Aims:

~To practise non-calculator arithmetic skills~

~To follow a complex set of instructions~

National Curriculum:

~Using and Applying Mathematics 1a; Number 1b, 3a, 3b~

Background:

~This activity shows you how to work out the day of the week for any date in the 20th century. Use it to impress your family and friends, but practise using the instructions first so that you are able to do the calculations quickly without a calculator.~

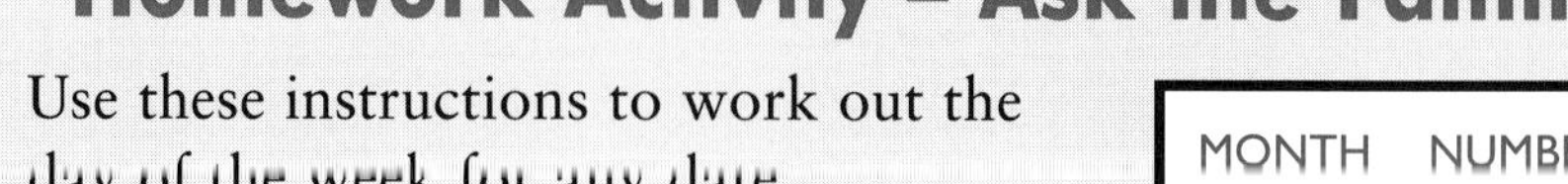

Homework Activity – Ask the Family

Use these instructions to work out the day of the week for any date.

MONTH	NUMBERS
January	1
February	4
March	4
April	0
May	2
June	5
July	0
August	3
September	6
October	1
November	4
December	6

1 Work out how many 12s will go into the last two digits of the year.

2 Work out the remainder in step 1.

3 Work out how many times 4 will go into the remainder.

4 Add the answers from steps 1, 2 and 3. If the answer is greater than 7, work out the remainder when divided by 7.

5 Add the month number (see table) to the answer from step 4.

6 Work out the remainder when the day of the month is divided by 7. Add this to the answer from step 5.

7 The answer from step 6 tells you the day of the week. 0 is Saturday, 1 is Sunday, 2 is Monday, and so on to Friday which is 6.

If the year is a leap year (leap years are divisible by 4 so the last two digits are 04, 08, 16, 20, 24, ..., 96) and the month is January or February, go back one day.

EXAMPLE USING 15TH OCTOBER 1957 (15/10/57)

1 57 divided by 12 is 4.

2 Remainder is 9.

3 9 divided by 4 is 2.

4 4 + 9 + 2 = 15 (more than 7, so divide by 7 to get remainder 1).

5 Add the month number (1) to get 2.

6 Day of month (15th) divided by 7 gives remainder 1. Final answer is 3.

7 1957 is not a leap year so 3 is Tuesday.

Ask people at home to choose birth dates, dates of weddings, historic dates etc, and you work out the day of the week for them.

MUM'S THE WORD

Homework Activity

Can you spot what is special about these three words?

ROTATOR MUM STATS

If you can't work it out then look up the word *palindrome* in a dictionary.

Palindromes do not have to be words and sentences.

The number 49394 is a palindrome.

Try to find ...

1 A palindrome greater than 100 which is a multiple of seven.
2 A palindrome which is a square number.
3 A palindrome greater than 100 which is prime.
4 A palindrome which is a multiple of 12.
5 Two palindromes whose difference is 2.
6 Two palindromes which add to give a palindrome.
7 Two palindromes whose difference is ten.
8 Two palindromes which multiply to give a palindrome.

~ Ask the family ~

See if someone at home can spot what is special about the palindromic words shown above. Ask them if they know any other palindromic words or sentences. Write them down and bring them in to school. Do any of your friends or relatives have palindromic telephone numbers or house numbers?

Aim:

~To use your knowledge of the number system to find certain types of number~

National Curriculum:

~Using and Applying Mathematics 1a, 2a, 3a; Number 2a, 3a~

Background:

~Are you still trying to work out what the title of this activity means? 'Mum' is a word with a special property and many numbers have the same property. You will find out about these numbers in this activity.~

WAS IT A CAT I SAW?

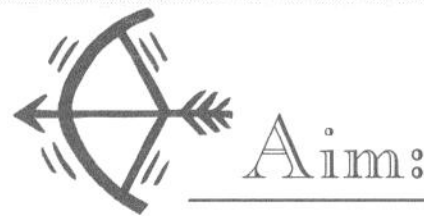

Aim:

~To carry out an investigative piece of number work~

National Curriculum:

~Using and Applying Mathematics 1a, 1b, 2a, 3a; Number 1b~

Background:

~If you haven't worked out what's special about the title, go back and read ***Mum's the Word*** *on page 15. You will come across* ***palindromes*** *again in the activities on this page.~*

Homework Activity

Choose any number.

Reverse the digits and add to the number.

Keep repeating this until you get a palindrome.

Example: 4075 + 5704 = 9779

4075 produces a palindrome after 1 addition.

Example: 268 + 862 = 1130 1130 + 0311 = 1441

268 produces a palindrome after 2 additions.

Start with 3897. How many additions are needed to produce a palindrome?

Find starting numbers which produce palindromes after 1 addition, 2 additions, 3 additions, 4 additions, 5 additions etc.

Are all of these possible?

What is the largest number of additions that are needed to produce a palindrome?

~ Ask the family ~

Try this 'mind-reading' trick with someone at home. Ask them to:

- write down any 3-figure number (all three digits different)
- reverse the digits to produce another 3-figure number
- subtract the smaller number from the larger
- reverse the digits of the answer and add this number to the answer.

Surprise them by telling them the answer. It will always be 1089.

You could ask them to make further calculations, for example: "Add 11 and then double the answer. Your answer is 2200."

A YEAR TO REMEMBER?

Homework Activity – Ask the Family

- Choose a year, for example the year that you were born, or use a year that has been chosen by someone at home.
- Use the four digits to write arithmetic questions that give an answer of one, two, three, four, five and so on, up to 100.
- Each digit can be used no more than once in each question.
- You can use any arithmetical operations and symbols that you know about, for example brackets, square roots, powers, fractions notation, and so on.

Here is an example using 1975.

$7 - 5 - 1 = 1$

$(9 + 1) \div 5 = 2$

$5 + 7 - 9 = 3$

$(7 \times 5 + 1) \div 9 = 4$

$15 \div \sqrt{9} = 5$

$(51 - 9) \div 7 = 6$

$19 - 7 - 5 = 7$

$\sqrt{9 \times 7 + 1} = 8$

and so on up to 100.

It might not be possible to make all of the answers from 1 to 100 but try to get as many as you can.

Make sure you understand the ones done by other people at home.

Aims:

~To practise a wide range of arithmetic skills~

~To use numbers and symbols in the right order~

~To understand how to use brackets in number work~

National Curriculum:

~Using and Applying Mathematics 1a, 1b, 2a, 3a; Number 1b, 2a, 3b, 4a, 4b~

Background:

~You get lots of practice at working out the answers to questions. In this activity you know the answers but have to work out the questions. Work on it with someone at home.~

BROKEN CALCULATOR KEYS

Aims:

~To understand some of the common calculator functions and the relationships between them~

~To find your own way of solving a problem~

National Curriculum:

~Using and Applying Mathematics 1a, 1b, 2a, 4a; Number 1a, 1b, 2a, 3e, 4a, 4b~

Background:

~It is unlikely that the square root button on your calculator will ever be broken, but it is important that we do not take functions like this for granted. This activity gets you to think about the arithmetic that lies behind some of the common calculator functions.~

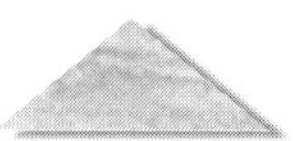

Homework Activity

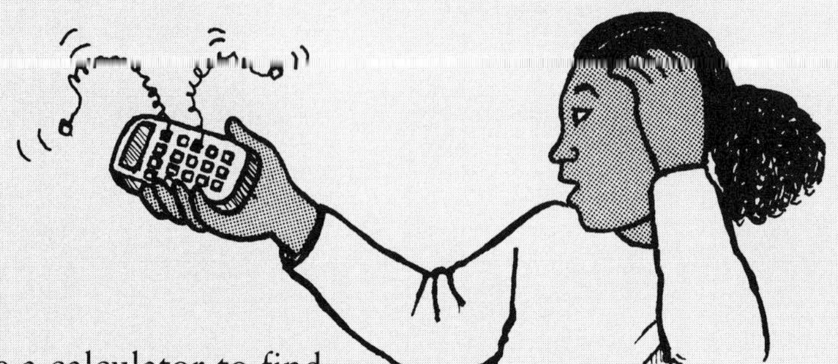

Use a calculator to find accurate answers to these problems.

The only calculator operations you are allowed to use are

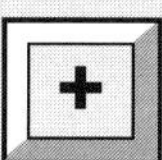 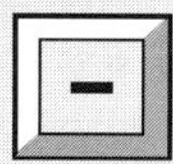   

You must not use the square root button, the cube root button or any mathematical or scientific functions. You can use the memory to store numbers if you want to.

1 A square has an area of 40 square centimetres. Work out the length of the sides.

2 A cube has a volume of 100 cubic centimetres. Work out the length of the sides.

3 Work out 37 ÷ 14 without using the division key.

4 Work out 4.75 x 2.836 without using the multiplication key.

5 Work out 5.9 x 1.45 without using the decimal point key.

For each problem explain in a few words how you worked out the answer.

~ Ask the family ~

Show these problems to someone at home.

Ask them how they would have done each one.

If they are not sure then you can explain it to them.

NUMBER CHAINS

Homework Activity

Choose a starting number less than 100.

Use these rules to work out the next number in the chain:

If the previous number is even, divide it by 2.

If the previous number is odd, add 1 to it.

Keep going until you get to 1.

Here is an example of a number chain which starts with 17.

17 is odd so add 1 to get 18.

18 is even so divide by 2 to get 9.

9 is odd so add 1 to get 10.

10 is even so divide by 2 to get 5.

And so on ...

Stop when you get 1.

17 18 9 10 5 6 3 4 2 1

This number chain has ten numbers.

Try to find the longest possible number chain.

Remember, your starting number must be less than 100.

~ Ask the family ~

Show someone at home what you have done.
Explain to them how you eventually found the longest chain.
Tell them how you decided which starting numbers to use.
Did you just pick any number or did you think carefully about it?

What do you notice about the last three numbers in all of your chains?

Ask the other person and see if they can spot it.

Aims:

~To follow a set of instructions~

~To use trial and improvement methods~

~To investigate a number problem in a logical way~

National Curriculum:

~Using and Applying Mathematics 1a, 1b, 2a, 3c, 4a; Number 1b~

Background:

~In mathematics it is important that we are able to follow rules and instructions. This activity asks you to follow a set of instructions but also gives you the freedom to choose your own way of solving the problem.~

NUMBER CHAIN DIAGRAMS

Aims:

~ To follow a set of instructions

~ To investigate a number problem in a logical way

~ To present mathematics work clearly and neatly ~

National Curriculum:

~Using and Applying Mathematics 1a, 1b, 2a, 3c, 3e; Number 1b~

Background:

~A clear, neat diagram is a very effective way of presenting mathematical information. This activity looks at one particular type of diagram and asks you to design and produce one of your own. You must do the ***Number Chains*** *activity on page 19 before doing this one.~*

Homework Activity

1 The diagram below shows the number chains for all starting numbers from 1 to 30.

For example, if you start with 27 you get the chain 27, 28, 14, 7, 8, 4, 2, 1.

The diagram also shows how one chain can be linked to another.

For example, if you start with 25 you get the chain 25, 26, 13, 14, 7, 8, 4, 2, 1.

This chain can be linked to the 27 chain as shown in the diagram.

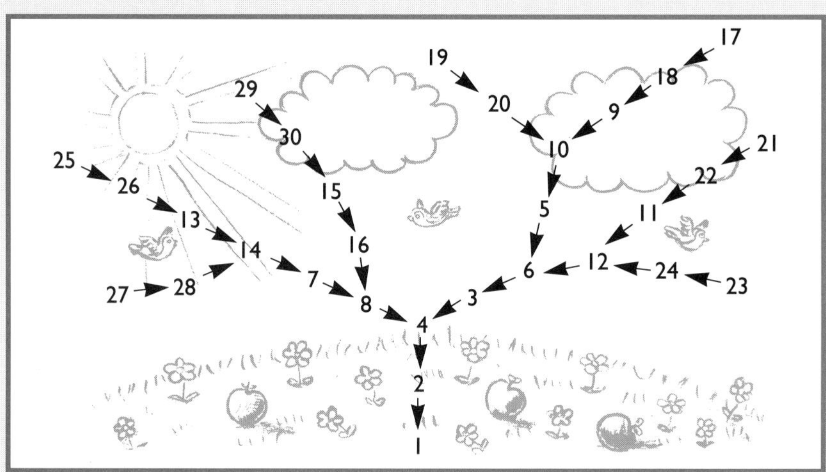

2 Produce a diagram which shows the number chains for all starting numbers from 1 to 100. Every number from 1 to 100 should appear on the diagram once and only once. You will have to plan your work carefully and may have to do it in rough first before producing a final version.

~ Ask the family ~

Show your diagram to someone at home and explain it to them. They might be able to suggest ways in which it could be improved.

MORE NUMBER CHAINS

Homework Activity

Choose a starting number less than 100.

Add the two digits together and then add to the number itself.

This gives you the next number in the chain.

Here is an example of a number chain which starts with 73.

73 → 83 → 94 → 7 → 14 → 19 → 29

The next number is 7 + 3 + 73 = 83.

The next number is 8 + 3 + 83 = 94.

The next number is 9 + 4 + 94 = 107.

If the answer is greater than 100 then subtract 100 so the next number is 7 rather than 107.

The next number is 7 + 7 = 14.

The next number is 1 + 4 + 14 = 19

And so on...

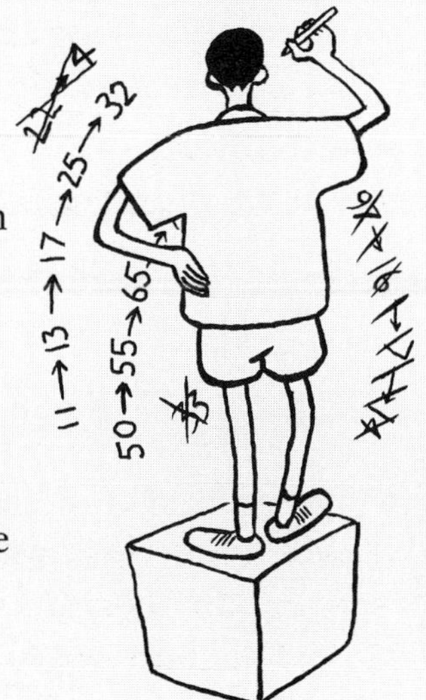

Produce a diagram which shows the number chains for all starting numbers from 1 to 100. Your diagram should show the links that exist between the chains. Every number from 1 to 100 should appear on the diagram once and only once. You will have to plan your work carefully and may have to do it in rough first before producing a final version.

~ Ask the family ~

Show your diagram to someone at home and explain it to them. They might be able to suggest ways in which it could be improved.

Aims:

~To follow a set of instructions~

~To investigate a number problem in a logical way~

~To present mathematics work clearly and neatly~

National Curriculum:

~Using and Applying Mathematics 1a, 1b, 2a, 3c, 3e; Number 1b~

Background:

*~In mathematics you need to be able to follow rules and instructions and also need to be able to set out your results clearly and neatly. This activity asks you to do all of these important things. It would be useful if you have already done the **Number Chains** and **Number Chain Diagrams** activities on pages 19 and 20.~*

THE BEST THINGS IN LIFE ARE FREE!

Aim:

~To calculate using percentages~

National Curriculum:

~Using and Applying Mathematics 1a, 3d; Number 1b, 2b, 3c~

Background:

~Percentages crop up on supermarket shelves and in your cupboards at home, so it is important to understand how they are being used. This activity asks you to check some of the figures that appear on various food products.~

Homework Activity

1 Let's check the figures on this box of cereal.

33% of 750g is 247.5g

So the special offer box should contain 750g + 247.5g = 997.5g

Why do you think there is a slight error?

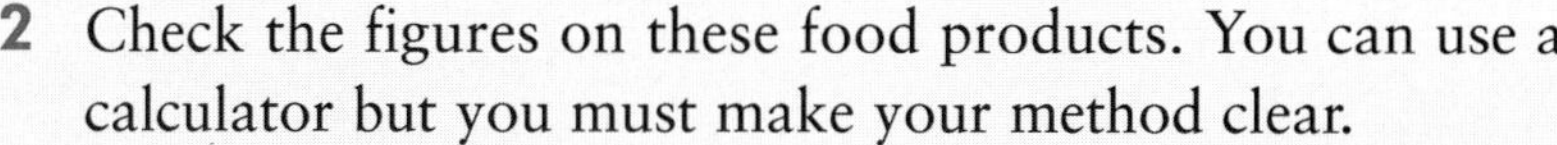

Does the 1kg box contain an extra 33%?

2 Check the figures on these food products. You can use a calculator but you must make your method clear.

- Box of breakfast cereal –
  33% extra free. 665g for the price of 500g.
- Can of cola –
  13% extra free. 500ml for the price of 440ml.
- Tin of new potatoes –
  40% extra free. 560g for the price of 400g.
- Bag of frozen cauliflower –
  50% extra free. 1.36kg for the price of 907g.
- Box of breakfast cereal –
  25% extra free. 470g for the price of 375g

~ Ask the family ~

Work with someone at home to find at least five products which have a percentage extra free. You might need to visit a local shop or supermarket.

Work together to check the figures for each product. Write down all the information you find and any figures you work out.

BLUE CROSS DAY

Homework Activity

Addem's Department Store reduced everything by 25% in the summer sale. The last three days of the sale were Blue Cross Days and the *sale prices* were reduced by a further 10%.

Subbit's Department Store reduced everything by 10% in the summer sale and on the Blue Cross Days reduced the *sale prices* by a further 25%.

Which department store would you rather shop at?

Look in a catalogue or use advertisements from newspapers and magazines to find the normal prices of five items that you would like to buy.

For each item work out the price on Blue Cross Day at Addem's and at Subbit's.

You can use a calculator but you must make your method clear and write down all of the figures you work out.

~ Ask the family ~

Tell people at home about the Blue Cross Days at Addem's and Subbit's but don't tell them about your calculations just yet.

Ask them which store they would rather shop at and why.

Ask as many people as you can.

Afterwards explain to them what you have found out. You might need to show them your calculations.

Aim:

~To calculate discounts using percentages~

National Curriculum:

~Using and Applying Mathematics 1a, 4a; Number 1a, 1b, 2b, 3c, 4b, 4d~

Background:

~Some shops seem to be having a sale every day of the year, so you need to know what you are doing if you want to get the best deal. This activity asks you to investigate sale prices.~

INTERESTING TIMES

Aims:

~To calculate using interest rates~

~To compare different types of savings account~

National Curriculum:

~Using and Applying Mathematics 1a, 2a, 4a; Number 1a, 1b, 2b, 3c, 4b, 4d~

Background:

~Interest rates are a common feature of everyday life, so it is important to understand that they can be calculated in various ways. This activity compares two different ways of earning interest in a savings account.~

Homework Activity

A bank offers a savings account with an **annual** interest rate of 12.5%. The interest is calculated and added to the account on the 31st December each year.

A building society offers a savings account with a **monthly** interest rate of 1%. The interest is calculated and added to the account on the last day of each month. Interest is paid on all money in the account, not just on the original amount paid in.

Suppose you had £100 to invest in a savings account. If you invested the money on the 1st January how much would you have by the end of the year if you used

- the bank?
- the building society?

Explain carefully how you worked out each answer.

~ Ask the family ~

Explain to someone at home how the bank and the building society calculate the interest and show them your calculations.

Ask them if they know how interest is calculated on any savings they might have. There might also be different ways of calculating interest to be paid on money that you borrow from a bank or building society. Look carefully at bank and building society advertisements in newspapers and see if they explain how the interest is calculated. You might be able to find out by picking up a leaflet from your local branch.

Make a note of anything you find out about interest rates and bring in to school any leaflets or advertisements you find.

CHOOSE YOUR PRIZE

Homework Activity

You have won first prize in the National Digest Prize Draw.

You can have either:

1 A lump sum of £100,000
2 £200 per week for the rest of your life
3 £1000 per month for the next 15 years
4 1p in the first year, 2p in the second, 4p in the third, 8p in the fourth, 16p in the fifth, and so on for the rest of your life.

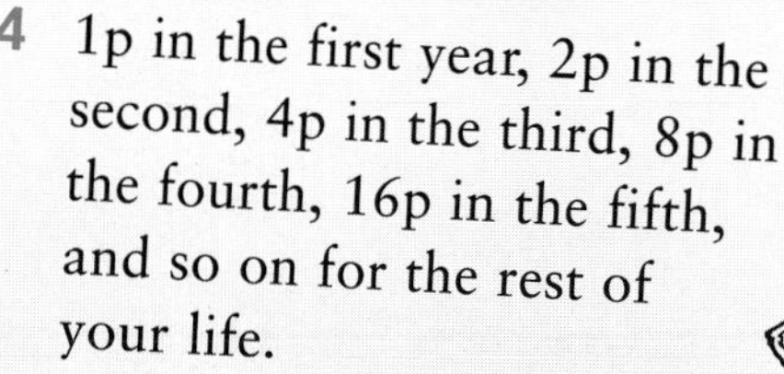

Which prize would you choose?

Explain carefully the reasons for your choice and show clearly any calculations you make.

~ Ask the family ~

Ask an adult at home which prize they would choose and get them to explain why.

Make a note of their choice and their reasons.

Ask a friend or a relative who is a lot older than you which prize they would choose.

Again, make a note of their choice and their reasons.

Aims:

~To practise arithmetic skills in the context of money~

~To be able to make a decision and justify it~

National Curriculum:

~Using and Applying Mathematics 1a, 1b, 3c, 4a; Number 1a, 1b, 4a, 4b~

Background:

~"Should I pay my bills monthly or quarterly?" "Is the large jar of coffee better value for money?" "Which savings account is best?" "What is the best way of paying for my new car?" These are just a few of the financial decisions that we all have to make during our lives. Some of us might even be lucky enough to have to make a decision like the one described in this activity.~

WHICH VIDEO TAPE?

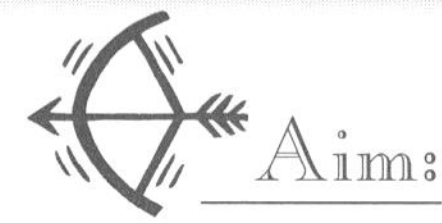

Aim:

~To compare products in terms of value for money~

National Curriculum:

~Using and Applying Mathematics 1a, 2a, 4a; Number 1b, 4a~

Background:

~Video tapes and audio cassettes come in various brands, sizes and prices but which one should we buy? This activity considers value for money but also asks you to discuss other factors that might be important.~

Homework Activity

Two common sizes of video tape are E180 and E240. What do the numbers mean? Ask someone at home if you are not sure.

A mail-order catalogue offers various packs of video tapes as follows:

3 x E180 tapes for £3.99

5 x E180 tapes for £6.99

11x E180 tapes for £14.99

2 x E180 tapes and
2 x E240 tapes for £8.99

3 x E240 tapes for £5.85

4 x E240 tapes for £8.99

8 x E240 tapes for £15.99

Arrange these seven packs in order starting with the one that is the best value for money and finishing with the worst.

You can use a calculator but make sure your method is clear and write down any figures you work out.

~ Ask the family ~

Find out what sorts of tapes people buy and what they cost. Compare these with the ones listed above. Are yours better value for money?

Explain what you have found out to someone at home. Ask them if they always buy the cheapest tapes or do they think that other factors are also important?

BIGGEST IS BEST?

Homework Activity

1 Tins of a particular brand of soup are available in three sizes. A 300g tin costs 41p, a 405g tin costs 48p and an 800g tin costs 79p. Which tin is the best value for money?

Explain your answer carefully and show any working out clearly.

2 Choose a particular brand of a product which is available in at least two different sizes. For each size find out how much you get and for what price. You might need to visit a local supermarket to find this information.

Work out which size is the best value for money.

Explain your answer carefully and show any working out clearly.

~ Ask the family ~

Explain your findings to someone at home.

Ask them if they ever work out which size is the best value for money when they go shopping.

Do they always buy the size which is the best value for money?

Is value for money the only consideration or are other things also important?

Make a note of the things you discuss.

Aims:

~To compare products in terms of value for money~

~To identify other important factors when purchasing various products~

National Curriculum:

~Using and Applying Mathematics 1a, 2a, 4a; Number 1b, 4a~

Background:

~Many products in supermarkets are available in different sizes and so it is important to be able to compare one size with another. Value for money is often a major consideration but sometimes it is not the only one. These themes are explored in this activity.~

RECHARGE YOUR BATTERIES

Aim:

~To make comparisons involving money and time~

National Curriculum:

~Using and Applying Mathematics 1a, 2a, 4a; Number 1b, 4a, 4b~

Background:

~Do you use rechargeable batteries or have you ever thought about using them? In this activity you will consider whether or not they are worth a try.~

Homework Activity

A personal cassette player uses two AA batteries.

Two long-life alkaline batteries cost £1.75 and last for about 18 hours.

A battery charger and four rechargeable batteries costs £12.75.

Rechargeable batteries last for about 7 hours and then need recharging.

If someone uses their cassette player only very occasionally (say 1 hour a week) what sort of batteries should they use? Someone else uses their cassette player regularly (say 1 hour a day). What sort of batteries should they use?

Give reasons for both answers and show any figures you work out.

What sort of batteries would you use?

Again, give reasons and use figures.

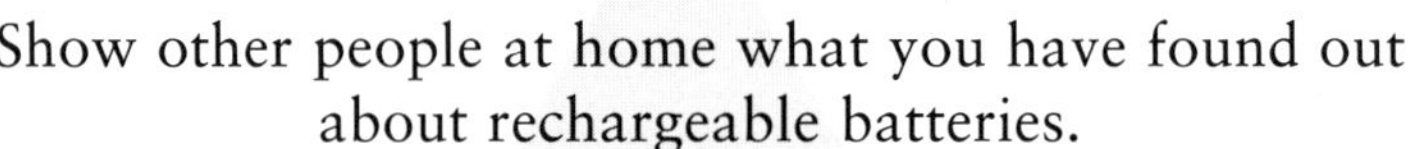

~ Ask the family ~

Show other people at home what you have found out about rechargeable batteries.

What would they use? Ask them to give reasons and make a note of what they say.

Is cost the only consideration or do they mention other things as well?

Look in a catalogue or visit a shop to find out the cost of long-life alkaline batteries and the cost of rechargeable batteries and a charger.

Are the prices mentioned above about right?

SYMMETRY SIGNS

Homework Activity

The local swimming pool used to be open every day of the week but just recently it stopped opening on Mondays. The manager of the pool put up this sign in the main entrance.

What is special about this sign?

(Hint: the other day the sign fell down and the receptionist put it back upside down, but nobody noticed.)

Design and make a sign or poster which has the same symmetrical properties as the swimming pool sign.

~ Ask the family ~

Show the swimming pool sign to someone at home and see if they can spot what is special about it.

Show them your sign or poster.

They might be able to suggest additional things that could be included on it or you could make another sign or poster together.

Aims:

~To understand and recognise rotational symmetry~

~To produce a sign or poster with a particular type of symmetry~

National Curriculum:

~Using and Applying Mathematics 1a, 3c; Shape, Space and Measures 1a, 1b, 2c, 3b~

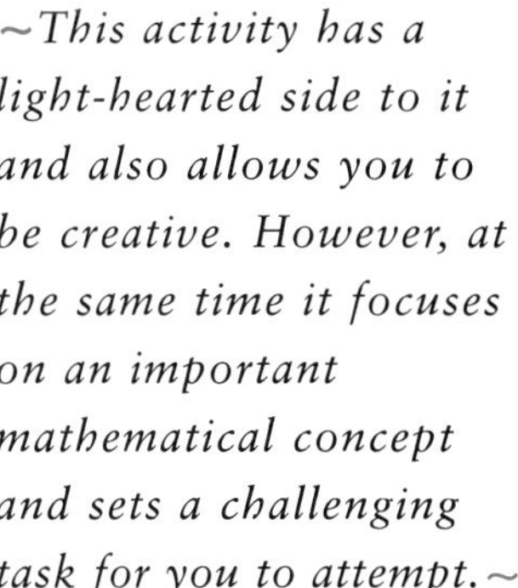

Background:

~This activity has a light-hearted side to it and also allows you to be creative. However, at the same time it focuses on an important mathematical concept and sets a challenging task for you to attempt.~

BACK TO FRONT

Aims:

~To understand and recognise a certain type of transformation~

~To produce a sign with a particular type of symmetry~

National Curriculum:

~Using and Applying Mathematics 1a, 3c; Shape, Space and Measures 1a, 1b, 2c, 3b, 3c~

Background:

~Have you ever wondered why some vehicles have back-to-front writing on them? No, the sign-writer did not make a mistake. There is a good reason and it can be explained mathematically.~

Homework Activity

1 You might have seen vehicles with signs like this on the front.

What would you have to do to these signs to make them appear to be the right way round? Describe this as fully and clearly as possible.

2 Transform this sign so that the words are back-to-front just like the ones above.

BACK TO FRONT

Describe fully and clearly the transformation that you carry out.

3 Try to find words which look exactly the same after this transformation as they did before it. In other words, the transformation has no effect on these words.

~ Ask the family ~

Show someone at home the signs on this page and the ones that you have drawn.

Together, try to think of other examples of back-to-front writing that you have seen.

Talk about the reasons why vehicles have back-to-front writing on them.

NOT DOMINOES – PENTOMINOES!

Homework Activity

A *pentomino* is a shape made by shading in five connected squares on a piece of squared paper. The squares must be connected along their edges, not just at the corners.

This is not a pentomino because two of the squares are not connected along an edge.

This is not a pentomino because the edges must connect along the entire side of a square.

This is a pentomino.

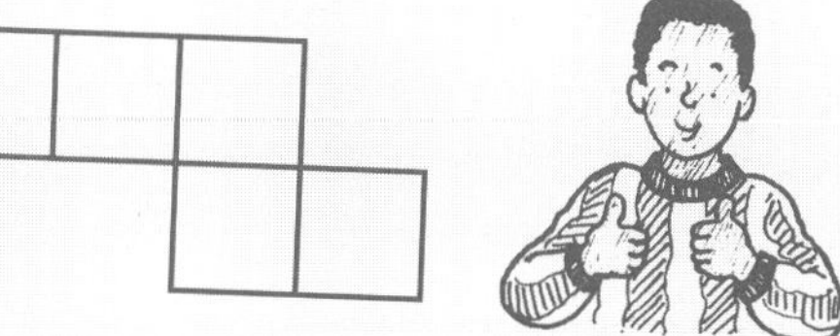

On squared paper draw as many different pentominoes as possible. You should be able to find more than ten.

~ Ask the family ~

Show your work to someone at home.

Do they think your pentominoes are all different, or perhaps they think some look the same?

Talk about what you mean by 'the same' or 'different'.

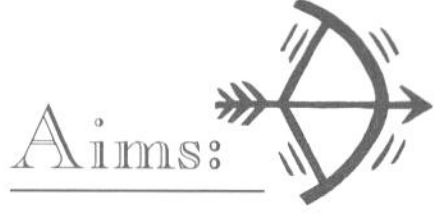

Aims:

~To investigate a shape problem in a logical way~

~To think about what we mean by 'the same' and 'different' when we are talking about shapes~

National Curriculum:

~Using and Applying Mathematics 1a, 3c, 4a; Shape, Space and Measures 1b, 2a, 2b, 3b~

Background:

~We use expressions such as 'the same' and 'different' in everyday language, but in mathematics we often need to be more precise than this. If we say that two shapes are 'different', what exactly do we mean?~

SORT IT OUT

Aims:

~To recognise line and rotational symmetry~

~To sort shapes according to their symmetry~

National Curriculum:

~Using and Applying Mathematics 1a, 2a, 3c, 3e; Shape, Space and Measures 2c~

Background:

~Line and rotational symmetry are two very important geometrical properties that can be seen all around us in both natural and man-made objects. This activity looks at the symmetrical properties of the pentominoes produced earlier. You must do the **Not Dominoes – Pentominoes!** activity on page 31 before attempting this one.~

Homework Activity

Which of the 12 pentominoes have exactly one line of symmetry ?

Which ones have exactly two lines of symmetry?

Which ones have three, four or five lines of symmetry?

Which pentominoes have rotational symmetry?

Shapes can have one, two, three, or more lines of symmetry, but are there different types of rotational symmetry?

Do any pentominoes have a line of symmetry but no rotational symmetry? Do any have rotational symmetry but no lines of symmetry?

Produce a diagram which sorts or classifies all of the pentominoes according to their symmetrical properties. Every pentomino should appear somewhere on the diagram.

~ Ask the family ~

Show your sorting diagram to someone at home and explain it to them. You might have to tell them about line and rotational symmetry.

Does your diagram make sense to them?

If your diagram is not clear then talk about ways of improving it and then make the improvements.

FIVE GO BOXING

Homework Activity

This is one of the 12 pentominoes.

This shape could be made out of card and folded to make an open-topped cube-shaped box.

Square E would be the bottom of the box and squares A, B, C and D would form the sides.

	A	
D	E	B
	C	

We say that the flat shape is the *net* of the open-topped box.

Look closely at the other 11 pentominoes.

Which ones are nets of the open-topped cube-shaped box?

If you are not sure, you might need to draw some of the pentominoes on paper, cut them out and try to fold them to make a box.

Choose the net that you think is the most unusual.

Draw it accurately on card, cut it out and then fold it to make the box.

~ Ask the family ~

Show your pentominoes to someone at home.
Ask them which ones they think will fold to make a box.
Tell them whether they are right or not.

Together, try to find an unusual piece of packaging at home which will fold flat easily. Bring it in to school.

Aims:

~To identify 2-D shapes that will fold to make a 3-D shape~

~To draw a 2-D shape and then fold it to make a 3-D shape~

National Curriculum:

~Using and Applying Mathematics 1a, 3a, 3c; Shape, Space and Measures 1a, 1b, 2a, 2b~

Background:

~Many of the three-dimensional boxes and containers that we see all around us started out as flat pieces of paper or card. Manufacturers have developed some very interesting ways of packaging the goods we buy. This activity looks at the relationship between 2-D and 3-D shapes. You must do the ***Not Dominoes – Pentominoes!*** *activity on page 31 before attempting this one.~*

GIMME FIVE!

Aim:

~To work in an investigative way involving number~

National Curriculum:

~Using and Applying Mathematics 1a, 2a, 4a, 4b, 4c, 4d; Number 1b~

Background:

~This activity provides important addition practice but, more importantly, you will have to make decisions, look for patterns and try things out for yourself.~

Homework Activity

If you don't know what a *pentomino* is, go back and read page 31.

A 100-square is a 10 by 10 grid showing the numbers 1 to 100. Here are the first few rows of a 100-square.

1	2	3	4	5	6	7	8	9	10
11	12	13	14	15	16	17	18	19	20
21	22	23	24	25	26	27	28	29	30
31	32	33	34	35	36	37	38	39	40
41	42	43	44	45	46	47	48	49	50

A pentomino will cover five numbers on a 100-square.

The pentomino shown above has a total of 135.

1 What happens to the total if you move the pentomino one square up? ... one square down? ... one square to the left? ... one square to the right?

2 Choose one of the pentominoes and position it on a 100-square so that its total is 200. Draw it and write the numbers in the squares. Is it possible to have more than one pentomino with a total of 200? If so, draw as many as you can find.

3 What is the biggest pentomino total you can have on a 100-square? ... what is the smallest?

4 Is it possible to make all of the pentomino totals between the smallest and the biggest or are some totals impossible? Explain your answer carefully.

~ Ask the family ~

Explain pentomino totals to someone at home. They may be able to help you to find some of the totals.

FIVE GO TILING

Homework Activity

If you don't know what a *pentomino* is, go back and read page 31.

This diagram shows that many copies of a single pentomino can be fitted together to cover a flat surface. The shapes fit together exactly with no gaps in between.

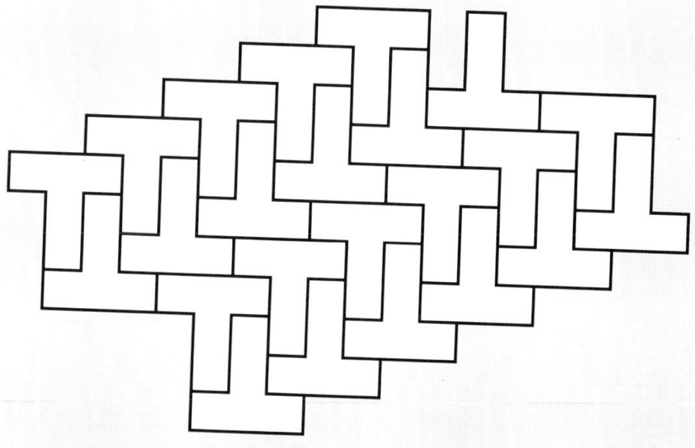

We say that this shape will *tessellate*.

The pattern that has been produced is called a *tessellation*.

Choose one of the pentominoes and see if you can produce a tessellation.

Draw it carefully on squared, plain or square spotty paper.

Aims:

~To understand the meaning of 'tessellate' and 'tessellation'~

~To produce a tessellation using a single repeated shape~

National Curriculum:

~Using and Applying Mathematics 1a, 3a, 3c, 4b; Shape, Space and Measures 1b, 2a, 3c~

Background:

~This shape investigation provides an opportunity to show your creative talents and also learn about an important mathematical concept.~

~ Ask the family ~

Explain tessellations to someone at home.

Together look at all the 12 pentominoes and decide which ones will tessellate and which ones will not.

Make a note of your decisions and give reasons for them.

DIY TILING

Aims:

~To produce an original tessellation~

~To be aware of tessellations that exist around us~

National Curriculum:

~Using and Applying Mathematics 1a, 3a, 3c; Shape, Space and Measures 1a, 1b, 2a, 3c~

Background:

~Tessellating with squares, rectangles, triangles and hexagons is easy. This activity shows how to tessellate using shapes which are much more interesting. Important connections are also made between mathematics and the world around us.~

Homework Activity

If you don't know what a *tessellation* is, look at the diagram on page 35 and read the explanation that goes with it.

Follow these instructions to produce an original and unusual tessellation of your own.

1 Start with a shape which you know will tessellate, such as a square, rectangle, triangle, hexagon, etc. Make a cardboard cut-out of the shape.

2 Cut a piece out of one side and attach it on the opposite side using sticky tape. You can repeat this a number of times if you want.

3 Use your cut-out as a template to draw around. In this way you can produce a tessellation on a large sheet of paper.

~ Ask the family ~

Show your tessellation to someone at home and explain how you did it.

Together try to find examples of interesting tessellations. Possible sources are tiled floors and the patterns in wallpapers, carpets, curtains and other fabrics.

If you have an encyclopaedia or access to the Internet, find out about the work of the artist M.C. Escher.

DOT-TO-DOT WITH SEVEN SPOTS

Homework Activity

Your teacher will provide you with a sheet with a hexagonal arrangement of dots like this. You can also make these arrangements on triangular spotty paper.

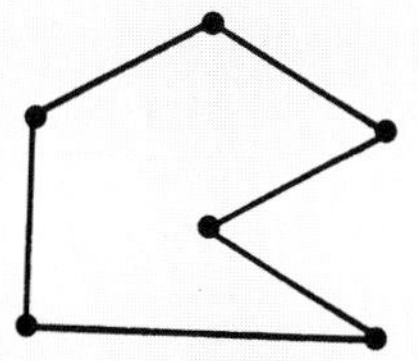

You can make seven-pin polygons by joining some or all of the seven dots (a polygon is an enclosed shape made from straight lines). Here is an example of a seven-pin polygon.

This is not a seven-pin polygon because it is in fact two shapes and one of the corners does not lie on a dot. Try to find as many different seven-pin polygons as you can. Record them on the paper provided by your teacher.

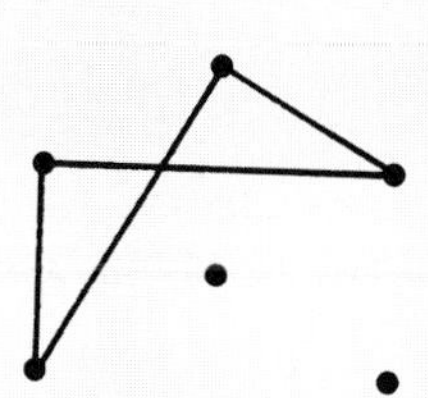

Many of the seven-pin polygons have mathematical names. Try to name as many of them as you can.

~ Ask the family ~

Show your seven-pin polygons to someone at home. Check them together to make sure that you have not drawn any of them twice. The other person might also spot some that you have missed out.

Aims:

~To carry out a shape investigation~

~To name various mathematical shapes~

National Curriculum:

~Using and Applying Mathematics 1a, 2d, 3a, 3c; Shape, Space and Measures 1b, 2a, 2b~

Background:

~This activity asks you to produce various shapes and to name as many of them as you can. But watch out – it is very easy to repeat some of the shapes if you are not careful!~

SEVEN-SPOT SYMMETRY

Aim:

~To recognise line and rotational symmetry~

National Curriculum:

~Using and Applying Mathematics 1a, 3c; Shape, Space and Measures 2c~

Background:

~This activity looks at the symmetrical properties of the seven-pin polygons produced earlier, as well as symmetry around us. You must do the ***Dot-to-Dot with Seven Spots*** *activity on page 37 before attempting this one.~*

Homework Activity

For each of your seven-pin polygons:

1 Draw any lines of symmetry.

2 Say whether or not it has rotational symmetry and, if it has, write down the *order* of rotational symmetry.

~ Ask the family ~

Show your seven-pin polygons to someone at home and explain line and rotational symmetry to them.

Together, try to find interesting examples of shapes that have line or rotational symmetry. Look at things such as labels on food products, company signs and logos, advertisements in newspapers and magazines, and so on.

Bring in to school or draw anything interesting that you find.

GUESS WHO? WITH SEVEN SPOTS

Homework Activity - Ask the family

Cut up your sheet of seven-pin polygons so that each one is on a separate piece of paper.

Lay the pieces of paper on a table so you can both see all of the seven-pin polygons.

Ask the other person to choose one of the seven-pin polygons without telling you which one it is.

You must ask the other person questions which have either a "yes" or a "no" answer.

Here are a few examples of questions you could ask:

"Does it have four sides?"

"Does it have exactly one line of symmetry?"

"Does it have a right-angle?"

Make a quick note of the questions you ask.

After the other person has answered "yes" or "no" each time, you should be able to remove some of the seven-pin polygons.

Eventually you should be able to work out which one was chosen by the other person.

DOES IT LOOK LIKE PACMAN?

Then it is your turn to choose one of the seven-pin polygons and the other person must try to work out which one it is. See who can do it with the fewest questions.

Aims:

~To identify the geometrical properties of various 2-D shapes~

~To use these properties in a logic game~

National Curriculum:

~Using and Applying Mathematics 1a, 2a, 3a; Shape, Space and Measures 2a, 2b, 2c, 2d~

Background:

~This game makes use of the shapes produced in the ***Dot-to-Dot with Seven Spots*** *activity on page 37. To play well, you will need to know the properties of 2-D shapes and also to think logically. Play the game with someone at home.~*

MORE TILING

Aims:

~*To understand the meaning of 'tessellate' and 'tessellation'*~

~*To produce a tessellation using a single repeated shape*~

National Curriculum:

~*Using and Applying Mathematics 1a, 3a, 3c, 4b; Shape, Space and Measures 1b, 2a, 3c*~

Background:

~*This activity looks at the important mathematical concept of* ***tessellation*** *by making use of the shapes produced in the* ***Dot-to-Dot with Seven Spots*** *activity on page 37.*~

Homework Activity

This diagram shows that many copies of a single shape can be fitted together to cover a flat surface. The shapes fit together exactly with no gaps in between.

We say that this shape will *tessellate*. The pattern that has been produced is called a *tessellation*. The tessellating shape above is one of the seven-pin polygons.

Choose one of the other seven-pin polygons and see if you can produce a tessellation. Be adventurous and try one of the more interesting ones! Draw it carefully on triangular spotty paper.

~ Ask the family ~

Explain tessellations to someone at home and show them what you have done.

Together, look at all the different seven-pin polygons and try to decide which ones will tessellate and which ones will not.

Make a note of your decisions and give reasons for them.

AREA WITH SEVEN SPOTS

Homework Activity

You will need to have done the *Dot-to-Dot with Seven Spots* activity on page 37 before attempting this one.

Look carefully at the shapes you produced in the earlier activity.

Assume that the small equilateral triangle has an area of 1 unit.

The area of the rhombus is therefore 2 units.

Use the same units to work out the areas of the other seven-pin polygons.

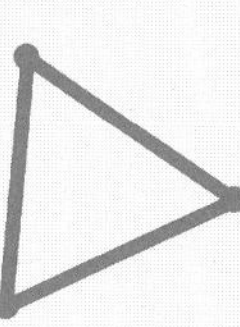

AREA = 2

~ Ask the family ~

Use a piece of triangular spotty paper to do this part of the activity with someone at home.

Assume that the area of the smallest equilateral triangle you can draw is 1 unit.

- Draw equilateral triangles with areas of 4, 9 and 16 units.
- Now try drawing equilateral triangles with areas of 3, 7 and 12 units.
- Use the same units to work out the areas of the rectangles that can be drawn on triangular spotty paper.

Aim:

~To work on problems involving area~

National Curriculum:

~Using and Applying Mathematics 1a, 1b, 2a, 3c; Shape, Space and Measures 1a, 1b, 2b, 4d~

Background:

~This activity looks at the areas of various shapes by using an unusual unit of measurement instead of square centimetres. You must do the ***Dot-to-Dot with Seven Spots*** *activity on page 37 before attempting this one.~*

ANGLES WITH SEVEN SPOTS

Aims:

~To identify and work out the internal angles of shapes~

~To investigate patterns and relationships involving angles~

National Curriculum:

~Using and Applying Mathematics 1a, 1b, 2a, 4c; Algebra 1a; Shape, Space and Measures 2d~

Homework Activity

One of the seven-pin polygons is a small equilateral triangle.

You should already know that the internal angles are all 60 degrees.

Many internal angles of other seven-pin polygons are multiples of 60 degrees. For example, the internal angle at point A is 2 x 60 degrees = 120 degrees.

The internal angle at point B is 5 x 60 degrees = 300 degrees.

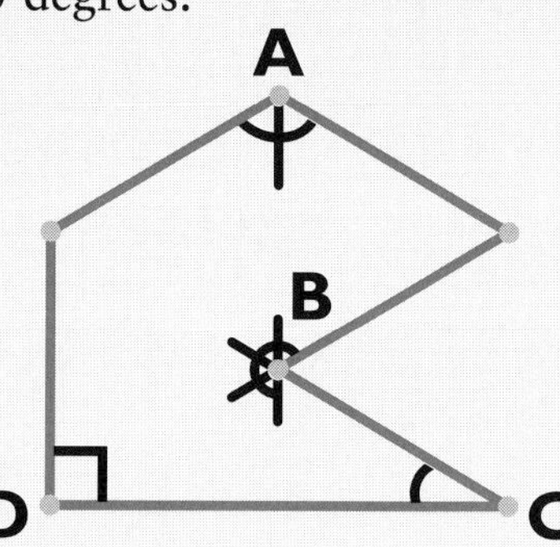

Some angles are half of 60 degrees. For example, the internal angle at point C is 30 degrees.

Some are right-angles, for example, the internal angle at point D.

1 Work out the internal angles of the seven-pin polygons and record these on your diagrams.

- For each seven-pin polygon, work out the sum of the internal angles.
- Can you spot a relationship between the number of sides a polygon has and the sum of its internal angles? Explain the relationship clearly in your own words.

ANGLES WITH SEVEN SPOTS

2 On triangular spotty paper draw shapes with eight, nine or ten sides and check to see if the relationship still exists. Show your working-out clearly.

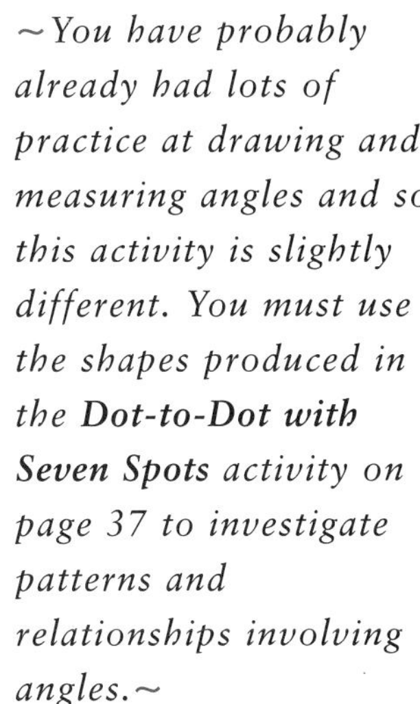

Background:

~You have probably already had lots of practice at drawing and measuring angles and so this activity is slightly different. You must use the shapes produced in the ***Dot-to-Dot with Seven Spots*** *activity on page 37 to investigate patterns and relationships involving angles.~*

~ Ask the family ~

Ask someone at home if they know what the sum of the angles in a triangle is.

What about squares, rectangles and shapes with more than four sides? Explain to them what you have discovered in this activity.

HOW MANY SQUARES?

Aims:

~To work in an investigative way involving shape~

~To find ways of working out areas~

National Curriculum:

~Using and Applying Mathematics 1a, 2a, 3c, 4a; Shape, Space and Measures 1b, 4d~

Background:

~You probably think that working out the area of a square is easy. That's exactly what you have to do here, but first you must find them!~

Homework Activity

Here is a ten by ten arrangement of dots.

Four dots can be used as corners and joined with straight lines to form a square.

The smallest possible square is a one by one square.

The biggest is a nine by nine square.

How many different squares can be drawn on a ten by ten arrangement of dots?

Note: *Different* means *different size*. The same square in a different position is not different.

Hint: There are more than nine different-sized squares.

Draw each square carefully on square spotty paper.

Work out the area of each square.

~ Ask the family ~

Show your squares to someone at home.

They might be able to spot some that you have missed.

Explain to them how you worked out the area of each square.

Together, can you think of any other ways of working out the areas of some of the squares?

Write down any alternative methods that you think of.

A GAME OF TWO HALVES

Homework Activity

There are many different ways of cutting a square in half.

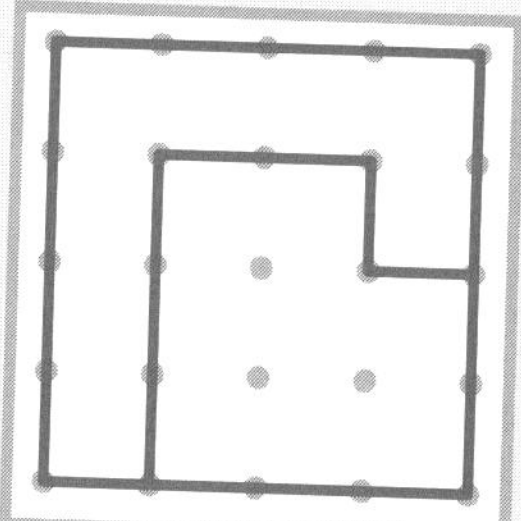

Here is one example. The two pieces have the same area but they are not the same shape. They are not *congruent*.

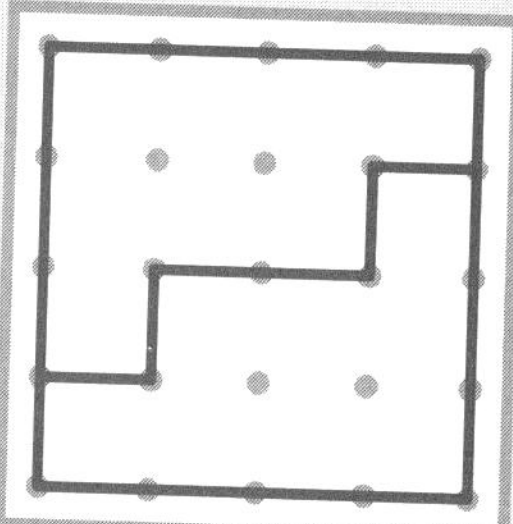

Here is another example. The two pieces have the same area and they are the same shape. They are *congruent*.

1 Find five different ways of dividing a square into two congruent halves.

2 Divide an equilateral triangle into two congruent halves.

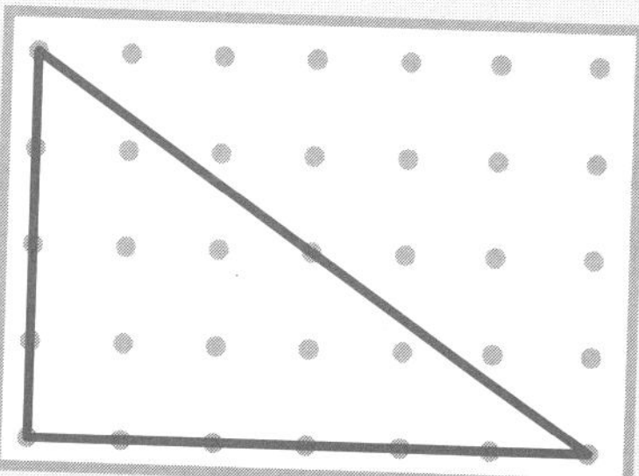

3 Can you divide this right-angled triangle into two congruent halves? Can you cut the right-angled triangle into three pieces and rearrange them to form two congruent shapes?

Make sure you show all of your answers clearly on paper.

Aim:

~To divide shapes into congruent pieces~

National Curriculum:

~Using and Applying Mathematics 1a, 2a, 3a, 3c; Shape, Space and Measures 1a, 1b, 2b~

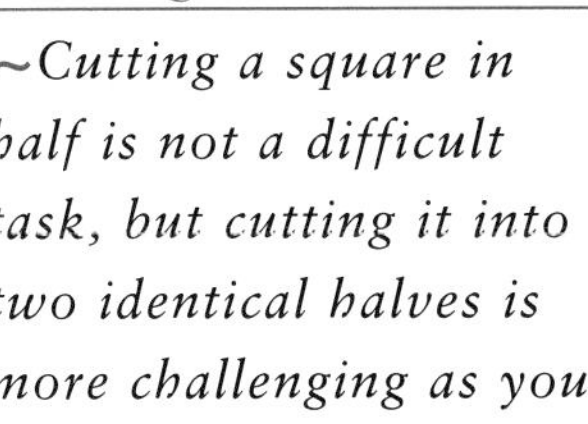

Background:

~Cutting a square in half is not a difficult task, but cutting it into two identical halves is more challenging as you will soon find out!~

~ Ask the family ~

Explain congruence to someone at home and show them your work.

They might be able to help you with some of your answers.

THIRDS AND QUARTERS

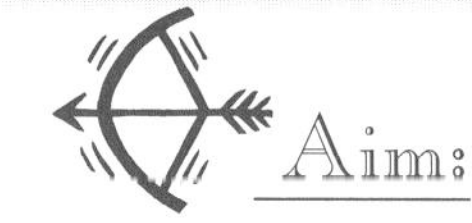

Aim:

~To divide shapes into congruent pieces~

National Curriculum:

~Using and Applying Mathematics 1a, 2a, 3a, 3c; Shape, Space and Measures 1a, 1b, 2b~

Background:

*~The activity **A Game of Two Halves** asks you to divide a square into two **congruent** halves. This time you have to divide various shapes into three or four **congruent** pieces.~*

Homework Activity

If you have forgotten what *congruent* means, go back and read page 45.

1 Divide a square into three congruent pieces.

2 Find two different ways of dividing an equilateral triangle into three congruent pieces.

3 Divide this 'L' shape into three congruent pieces

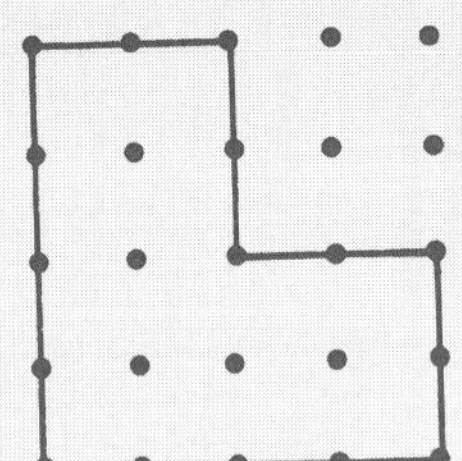

4 Divide this trapezium into three congruent pieces.

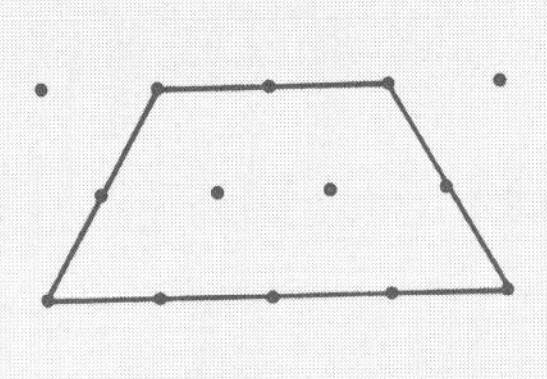

5 Find five different ways of dividing a square into four congruent pieces.

6 Divide an equilateral triangle into four congruent pieces.

7 Divide the 'L' shape into four congruent pieces.

8 Divide the trapezium into four congruent pieces.

9 Divide this right-angled triangle into four congruent pieces.

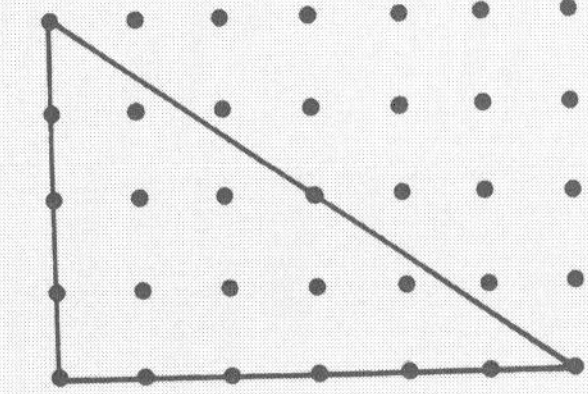

Make sure you show all of your answers clearly on paper.

~ Ask the family ~

Some of these questions are quite tricky. Explain congruence to someone at home and then ask them to try a few of the questions.

If there are any they can't do, show them your solution (if you were able to do it).

WHAT'S BETWEEN THE COVERS?

Homework Activity

1 Work out the area of the cover of this book in square centimetres.

2 If this book was cut up and all the pages laid out on a flat surface, what area would they cover? Give your answer in square centimetres and also in square metres.

3 Find a book at home or in the library which is bigger and has many more pages than this book. Work out the area that the pages would cover if they were laid out on a flat surface. You can use a calculator but your method must be clear.

4 Find something which is roughly the same area as the pages of the book. For example, it could be your bedroom floor, your back garden, a football pitch, or any other surface you can think of.

~ Ask the family ~

Show the book to someone at home. Ask them to choose a surface which is roughly the same as the area the pages would cover. You could give them a list of possible answers like this:

the kitchen table ~ the bedroom floor ~ the back garden.

Make sure you include something on the list which is roughly the same area as the pages of the book.

Ask as many people as you can.

Then tell them the answer and see if they were right.

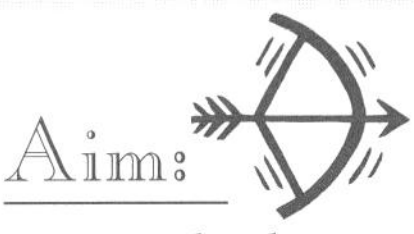

Aim:

~To calculate areas of rectangles using square centimetres and square metres~

National Curriculum:

~Using and Applying Mathematics 1a, 2a; Number 4a; Shape, Space and Measures 4a, 4d~

Background:

~This activity provides valuable practice at working out the areas of rectangles but also asks you to think about and compare the areas of everyday surfaces.~

MAKE IT BIG

Aims:

~To draw accurately various 2-D shapes~

~To work out areas and perimeters of 2-D shapes~

~To solve problems involving perimeter and area~

National Curriculum:

~Using and Applying Mathematics 1a, 1b, 2a, 2b, 3c, 4a; Shape, Space and Measures 1b, 2b, 4d~

Background:

~In mathematics you need to be able to work out the areas and perimeters of various shapes and also understand the relationship between these two important concepts. You can then apply what you know to real-life situations, as shown in this activity.~

Homework Activity

1 Draw accurately each of the following shapes and work out the area of each one:

(a) a rectangle with a perimeter of 24 centimetres

(b) a square with a perimeter of 24 centimetres

(c) a right-angled triangle with a perimeter of 24 centimetres

(d) an isosceles triangle with a perimeter of 24 centimetres

(e) an equilateral triangle with a perimeter of 24 centimetres

Find the shape with a perimeter of 24 centimetres that has the biggest possible area.

2 A farmer has eight straight lengths of rigid fencing, each three metres long, and uses them to make an animal enclosure in the middle of a large field.

- Draw the biggest enclosure he can make and work out its area.
- Explain why you think this is the biggest enclosure.

~ Ask the family ~

Briefly explain to someone at home the fencing problem and the solution you have come up with.

Together, think about and discuss these questions:

1 If you spill a small amount of liquid on a flat surface, what shape does it form?

2 Why are most pizzas, pies and burgers the shape that they are?

Do the answers have anything to do with the fencing problem?

FENCING PROBLEMS

Homework Activity

A farmer has 24 straight lengths of rigid fencing, each one metre long. He uses them to make a rectangular enclosure. An existing wall is used as one of the sides of the enclosure. The 24 lengths of fencing form the other three sides.

Here is a plan view of one possible enclosure. It has an area of 64 square metres. Find the enclosure with the biggest area.

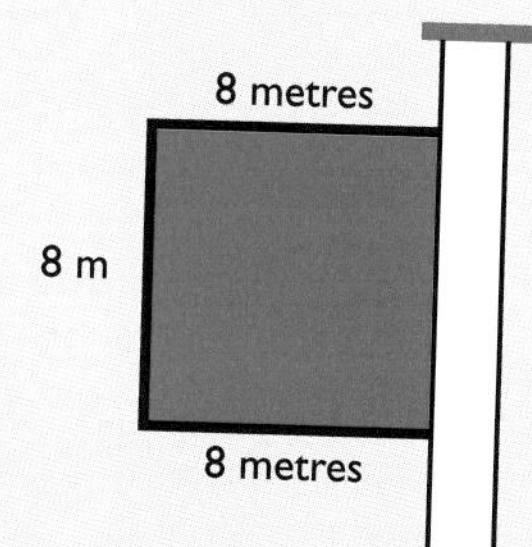

Suppose the farmer uses the 24 lengths of fencing and the existing wall in the corner of the field.

Here is one possible enclosure.

Find the enclosure with the biggest area.

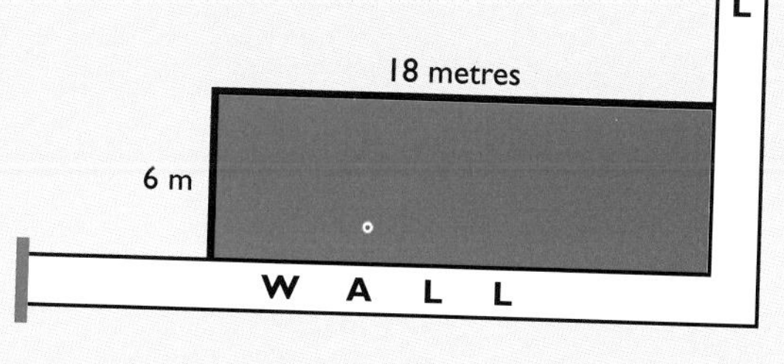

~ Ask the family ~

Briefly explain the first problem to someone at home.

Ask them what sort of enclosure they think will give the biggest area, for example a square one, a long thin one alongside the wall, a long thin one at right-angles to the wall, or perhaps a shorter, wider rectangle? Then tell them what you have found.

Do this again for the second problem.

Aim:

~To investigate problems involving areas and perimeters of rectangles~

National Curriculum:

~Using and Applying Mathematics 1a, 1b, 2a, 2b, 3c; Shape, Space and Measures 4d~

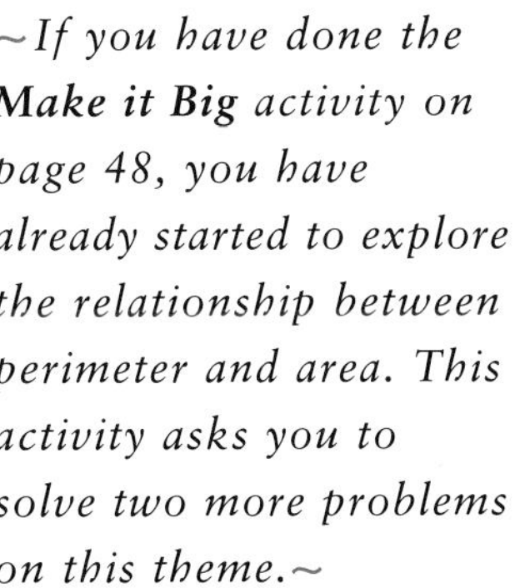

Background:

~If you have done the ***Make it Big*** *activity on page 48, you have already started to explore the relationship between perimeter and area. This activity asks you to solve two more problems on this theme.~*

MORE FENCING PROBLEMS

Aim:

~To investigate problems involving areas and perimeters~

National Curriculum:

~Using and Applying Mathematics 1a, 1b, 2a, 2b, 3c; Shape, Space and Measures 4d~

Background:

~It is assumed that you have already done ***Fencing Problems*** *on page 49, because this activity asks you to investigate these two problems further. Again, you have to find enclosures with the biggest area, but this time they do not have to be rectangular.~*

Homework Activity

1 A farmer has 24 straight lengths of rigid fencing, each one metre long. He uses them to make an enclosure.

An existing wall is used as one of the sides of the enclosure. The 24 lengths of fencing form the other sides. The enclosures can be any shape.

Here is a plan view of one possible enclosure (a right-angled triangle).

It has an area of $\frac{1}{2}$ x 12 x 12 = 72 square metres.

12 metres

12 metres

WALL

Find the enclosure with the biggest area. You can find the areas of your enclosures by making an accurate scale drawing or by calculation.

2 Suppose the farmer uses the 24 lengths of fencing and the existing wall in the corner of the field. Here is one possible enclosure (another right-angled triangle).

Find the enclosure with the biggest area.

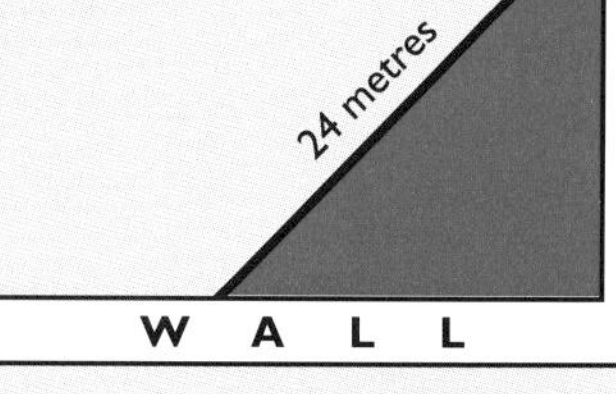

~ Ask the family ~

Briefly explain the first problem to someone at home.

Ask them what sort of shape they think will give the biggest area.

Then tell them what you have found.

Do this again for the second problem.

AREA AND PERIMETER: TRUE OR FALSE?

Homework Activity

Decide whether each of thc statements below is true or false.

You must use examples to support your answers.

1. Two rectangles have the same area so they must have the same perimeter.
2. Two rectangles have the same perimeter so they must have the same area.
3. It is not possible for the perimeter of a shape (in centimetres) to be the same as its area (in square centimetres).
4. You have two shapes. The one with the smallest area must also have the smallest perimeter.
5. The area of a shape is 10 square centimetres more than the area of another shape. The perimeter of the first shape is 10 centimetres more than the perimeter of the other shape. It is not possible to have two shapes like this.
6. The area of a shape is twice as big as the area of another shape. The perimeter of the first shape is twice as big as the perimeter of the other shape. It is not possible to have two shapes like this.

~ Ask the family ~

Show the six statements to someone at home.

Ask them to decide quickly whether each one is true or false.

Then explain to them what you think about each statement.

Aims:

~To prove that statements are true or false by using examples~

~To show an understanding of area and perimeter~

National Curriculum:

~Using and Applying Mathematics 1a, 1b, 1c, 2a, 2b, 3c, 4a, 4b, 4c, 4d, 4e; Shape, Space and Measures 1b, 4d~

Background:

~You have probably already had lots of practice at working out areas and perimeters of shapes. This activity is not so straightforward. You really have to think about area and perimeter and choose examples of your own to show whether certain things are true or false.~

DRASTIC MEASURES

Aims:

~*To appreciate the limitations of approximate answers and measurements*~

~*To know when to use approximations and when more precise figures should be used*~

National Curriculum:

~*Using and Applying Mathematics 1a; Number 2a, 4a, 4d; Shape, Space and Measures 4b, 4d*~

Background:

~*Other activities in this book show that it is not always necessary to give a precise answer or measurement. But there are times when a rough answer is not good enough.*~

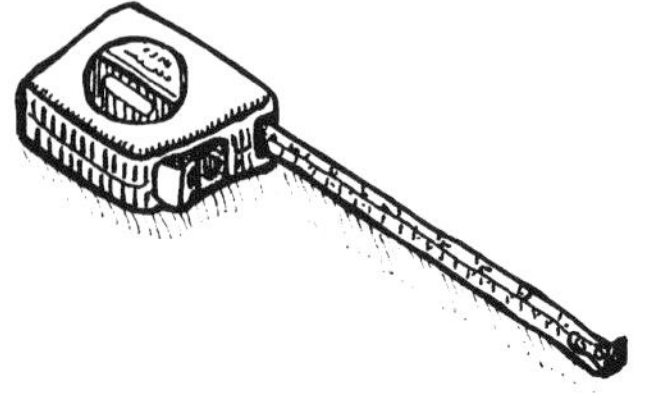

Homework Activity

1 A man wants to buy a new carpet for a rectangular room. Someone else has measured the room and tells him that it is 6 metres long by 4 metres wide (both distances to the nearest metre).

- What is the maximum possible true length of the room?
- What is the minimum possible true length?
- What is the maximum possible true width?
- What is the minimum possible true width?
- What is the maximum possible true area of the room?
- What is the minimum possible true area?

2 The man wants to buy carpet which costs £18.75 per square metre.

- What are the maximum and minimum possible costs of the carpet?
- If you were in this position, what would you do?

~ Ask the family ~

Choose a rectangular room in your home (ignore fireplaces and alcoves).

Ask someone at home to measure the length and width of the room to the nearest metre.

Use the approximate measurements to work out the maximum and minimum possible areas of the room.

Together, measure the room accurately and work out the true area.

Explain your calculations to the other person and show them what could happen if rough figures are used.

TIME FOR MUSIC

Homework Activity - Ask the family

1 Here are 11 tracks which appear on a 'Classical Music at the Movies' CD. The times are in minutes and seconds.

Classical Music at the Movies	
2001: A Space Odyssey	1.46
Platoon	6.21
My Left Foot	4.42
Die Hard 2	7.20
The Witches of Eastwick	3.11
Alien	8.02
Apocalypse Now	5.22
Fatal Attraction	5.11
Elvira Madigan	7.36
Gallipoli	7.42
Excalibur	2.45
Total Time	59.58

Suppose you wanted to copy the CD on to a C60 cassette. Sort the 11 tracks into a 'Side A' set and a 'Side B' set so that they will fit on to the C60 cassette.

2 Find a music CD or a computer CD-ROM.

Work out as accurately as you can the area of one side of the CD in square centimetres.

Show clearly any working out that you do, and also explain in a few sentences how you worked it out.

3 Find an audio cassette, for example a C60 or a C90.

Estimate as accurately as you can the length of the tape in the cassette in centimetres.

Show clearly any working out that you do, and also explain in a few sentences how you worked it out.

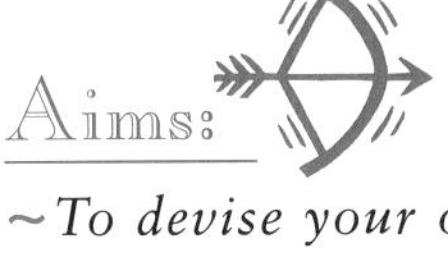

Aims:

~To devise your own methods of solving problems involving times, lengths and areas~

~To explain in your own words the methods used~

National Curriculum:

~Using and Applying Mathematics 1a, 1b, 2a, 4a; Shape, Space and Measures 4a, 4d~

Background:

~This activity asks you to work with someone at home to devise ways of solving three tricky problems involving everyday objects.~

ARE THEY SIMILAR?

Aims:

~To understand the mathematical meaning of the word 'similar'~

~To check to see if two shapes are similar or not~

National Curriculum:

~Using and Applying Mathematics 1a, 2a, 2b, 3a; Number 4a; Shape, Space and Measures 4a~

Background:

~We use the word 'similar' in everyday language but the mathematical meaning is slightly different. Two shapes are ***similar*** *in the mathematical sense if one is an enlargement of the other. This activity asks you to check to see if two shapes are mathematically similar.~*

Homework Activity

Some cans of drink are now available in two sizes.

The standard can is 11.2 cm tall and 6.4 cm in diameter.

The small can is 8.5 cm tall and 5.1 cm in diameter. Are the two cans similar, in other words, is one can an enlargement of the other?

Explain your answer carefully and show any working-out clearly.

~ Ask the family ~

Explain to someone at home what similarity means in the mathematical sense.

Together, find two or more objects around the home that look as if they might be similar. Possible examples include:

food products that are available in different sizes;

a set of saucepans that come in different sizes;

storage jars that come in different sizes.

Measure the dimensions of the objects and decide whether or not they are similar.

Explain your answer carefully and show any working-out clearly.

Together, try to think of other everyday examples of similar objects. Write down all of the examples you think of.

OLYMPICS '96 - WHO WON THE GOLD?

Homework Activity

Here are a few highlights from the 1996 Olympic Games in Atlanta.

1 In the high jump Steve Smith (GB) cleared 2.35 metres, while Charles Austin (USA) cleared 7 feet 10 inches.

Using the conversion 1 inch = 2.5 cm, work out who cleared the greater height.

A more accurate conversion is 1 inch = 2.54 cm. Use this to see who won the gold medal.

2 In the triple jump Jonathon Edwards (GB) jumped 17.88 metres, while Kenny Harrison (USA) jumped 59 feet 4 inches. Who won the gold medal and by what margin?

Give your answer in both metric and imperial units.

3 In the javelin Steve Backley (GB) threw a distance of 286 feet $10\frac{1}{2}$ inches, while his rival Jan Zelezny (Czech Rep.) threw 88.16 metres. Who won the gold medal and by what margin?

Give your answer in both metric and imperial units.

~ Ask the family ~

Ask people at home if they know their height in feet and inches.

Ask them if they know their height in metres or centimetres.

If they don't know then do the metric conversion together.

Try to ask as many people as possible including friends, relatives and neighbours.

What conclusions can you make? Do people tend to use imperial or metric measures?

Aims:

~To compare distances using metric and imperial units~

~To investigate whether people tend to use metric or imperial measures~

National Curriculum:

~Using and Applying Mathematics 1a, 2a; Number 1b, 2a, 4a; Shape, Space and Measures 4a~

Background:

~Both metric and imperial measures for distances are in everyday use. Many people know their height in feet and inches but not in metres. This activity asks you to compare metric and imperial distances and also to investigate what sorts of measures are used by people in your home.~

MILES, KILOMETRES AND FIBONACCI

Aims:

~To check the accuracy of an imperial to metric conversion method~

~To talk about other ways of converting between metric and imperial units~

National Curriculum:

~Using and Applying Mathematics 1a, 2b; Number 3d; Shape, Space and Measures 4a~

Background:

~Have you ever needed to quickly convert miles into kilometres or vice versa? This activity asks you to check the accuracy of an interesting conversion method.~

Homework Activity

Look carefully at this sequence of numbers.

1, 1, 2, 3, 5, 8, 13, 21, ...

Can you spot the pattern?

What are the next three numbers in the sequence?

This sequence is called the *Fibonacci sequence*, named after an Italian mathematician.

The sequence can be linked with many areas of mathematics but one of its uses is that it provides a rough way of converting miles into kilometres.

2 miles is approximately 3 kilometres.

3 miles is approximately 5 kilometres.

5 miles is approximately 8 kilometres.

8 miles is approximately 13 kilometres, and so on ...

Given that 1 mile = 1.6093 km, check the accuracy of the rough conversions provided by the Fibonacci sequence.

What errors do the rough conversions produce?

What are these errors as a percentage of the true figures?

Do the rough conversions get better or worse as you move further along the sequence? Overall, do you think this conversion method is worth using or not?

~ Ask the family ~

Explain the Fibonacci conversion method to someone at home.

Ask them if they know of any other quick ways of converting from metric to imperial measures or vice versa. These might involve distances, weights, volumes, capacities, and so on. Write down any conversions that they can think of.

LOADSA MONEY

Homework Activity

Imagine a pile of 2p coins, stacked one on top of the other, 100 metres high.

Also imagine 20p coins laid flat on the ground in a straight line 100 metres long.

Which would you rather have?

How much money would there be?

You can use a calculator but you must explain your method carefully and show any figures that you work out.

~ Ask the family ~

Ask people at home which arrangement of coins they would prefer.

Explain to them what you have found out.

Work with someone at home to answer this question:

What would you rather have, a tonne of £1 coins or a tonne of 20p coins?

How much money would there be?

Remember to explain your method clearly and show any figures you use. (Note: 1 tonne = 1000 kg.)

Aims:

~To measure distances and weights~

~To calculate using distances, weights and money~

National Curriculum:

~Using and Applying Mathematics 1a, 1b, 2a, 2b, 4a; Number 4a; Shape, Space and Measures 4a~

Background:

~Which weighs more, a tonne of lead or a tonne of feathers? We've all heard that one before, but what about this one:

Which is worth more, a tonne of £1 coins or a tonne of 20p coins?

You'll have to find out for yourself!~

OLYMPICS '96 - WEIGHTY PROBLEMS

Aims:

~To compare weights using metric and imperial units~

~To investigate whether people tend to use metric or imperial measures~

National Curriculum:

~Using and Applying Mathematics 1a, 2a; Number 1b, 2a, 4a; Shape, Space and Measures 4a~

Background:

~Shops and supermarkets weigh and price food using metric units of weight, but many people continue to use imperial measures. For example, many people know their weight in stones but not in kilograms. This activity asks you to compare metric and imperial weights and investigate what sorts of measures are used in your home.~

Homework Activity

Here are a few highlights from the 1996 Olympic Games in Atlanta.

1 In the shot put event the men's shot weighs 16 pounds (lbs).

How much heavier is this than the women's shot, which weighs 4 kilograms?

(Note: There are 16 ounces (oz) in 1 lb and 1 oz is 28 grams.)

2 The men's discus weighs 4 lb. $6\frac{1}{2}$ oz.

How much heavier is this than the women's discus, which weighs 1 kilogram?

3 The lightest Olympic boxing division is Light Flyweight for boxers weighing less than 48 kilograms.

What is this weight in stones and pounds?

(Note: There are 14 lb in 1 stone and 1 kilogram is 2.2 lb.)

~ Ask the family ~

Ask people at home if they know their weight in stones and pounds.

Ask them if they know their weight in kilograms.

If they don't know, then do the metric conversion together.

Try to ask as many people as possible including friends, relatives and neighbours.

What conclusions can you make? Do people tend to use imperial or metric measures?

THE DRIPPING TAP

Homework Activity - Ask the family

If you have a dripping tap in your home, use it for this activity. If you do not have a dripping tap, turn a tap on very slightly so that it does drip at a steady rate (about one drip per second should be fine).

1 Work with someone at home to find a way of measuring how much water is dripping from the tap. Work out how many litres of water would drip from the tap in a year.

Explain carefully how you measured the water and show all of your working-out clearly. You can use a calculator but you must make your method clear.

2 Would the wasted water from the dripping tap fill a bath during the year? Would it fill more than one bath? How many baths would it fill?

Again, explain your answers carefully and make your method clear.

Aims:

~To estimate, measure and calculate using volumes and capacities~

~To investigate a real-life household situation~

National Curriculum:

~Using and Applying Mathematics 1a, 2a, 2b, 4a; Number 1b, 4a; Shape, Space and Measures 4a, 4d~

Background:

~We tend to think of dripping taps as nothing more than a nuisance. But they are also a waste of valuable water. You might be surprised by how much water can be lost in this way.~

A BRICK IN THE TOILET

Aims:

~To estimate, measure and calculate using volumes and capacities~

~To investigate a real-life household situation~

National Curriculum:

~Using and Applying Mathematics 1a, 2a, 2b, 4a; Number 1b, 4a; Shape, Space and Measures 4a, 4d~

Background:

~In times of water shortage it has been suggested that a brick in the cistern of your toilet can save vast amounts of precious water. This activity asks you to investigate how much water can be saved in this way.~

Homework Activity - Ask the family

1 Work with someone at home to estimate the volume of water in the cistern of your toilet. If you have more than one toilet, then estimate the volume of all cisterns.

You can use a calculator but you must make your method clear. Also estimate the number of times your toilet (or toilets) is flushed each year. Again, you must make your method clear and explain any assumptions that you make.

How many litres of water are used in your home each year by flushing the toilet or toilets?

2 An ordinary building brick is 21.5 cm long, 10 cm wide and 7 cm tall. Assume that it is a cuboid and so does not have any holes or hollows in it. If you were to place a brick in the cistern of your toilet (or toilets) it would replace some of the water each time the cistern filled up. How much water would you save each year if you did this?

Make sure your methods and explanations are clear and can be followed by someone else reading your work.

WATER COUNTS

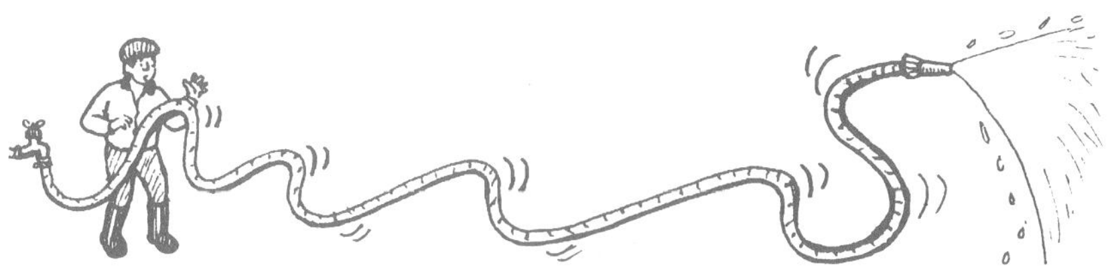

Homework Activity - Ask the family

Work with someone at home to estimate the total amount of water you use in your home during a year. You could start by making a list of all the ways that water is used in your home and then estimate the quantity for each.

The following information might be useful.

Typical Water Consumption Figures	
Having a bath	100 litres
A 5-minute shower	25 litres
Flushing the toilet	8 litres
Using the washing machine	70 litres
Using the dishwasher	35 litres
Using a hosepipe	9 litres per min.

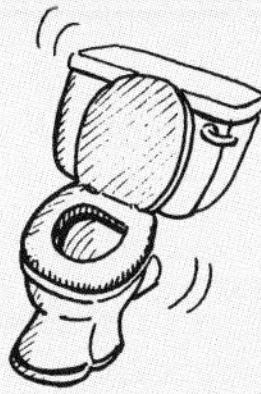

You should be able to think of many other ways that water is used in your home.

Show all of your figures and make it clear how you worked them out. If some of your figures are based on your own estimates, explain where these came from and state any assumptions that you made.

If a cuboid-shaped tank was built to hold all of the water that you use in a year, what would the dimensions of the tank be?

Aim:

~To estimate and calculate using capacities and volumes~

National Curriculum:

~Using and Applying Mathematics 1a, 1b, 2a, 2b, 3c, 4a; Number 1b, 4a; Shape, Space and Measures 4a, 4d~

Background:

~Do you have any idea how much water you use in a year or how much space all that water would take up? You are about to find out!~

ALL TANKED UP (BUT HOW FAR TO GO?)

Aim:

~To solve problems involving various measures~

National Curriculum:

~Using and Applying Mathematics 1a, 1b, 2a, 3c; Number 1b, 4a; Shape, Space and Measures 4c~

Background:

~How far can you drive on a tank of petrol? It will depend on how economical the car is, how much the tank will hold and perhaps other things as well.~

Homework Activity

Here are some figures for various types of cars.

Fuel Economy (miles per gallon)	
Ford Escort	39
Jaguar XJ8	23
Nissan Micra	49
Range Rover	18
Rover 600	33
VW Sharan	27

Size of Fuel Tank (litres)	
Ford Escort	55
Jaguar XJ8	81
Nissan Micra	42
Range Rover	100
Rover 600	65
VW Sharan	75

Work out how far (in miles) each car will travel on a full tank of petrol.

Use the conversion 1 litre = 0.2199 gallons.

You can use a calculator but you must make your method clear.

~ Ask the family ~

If someone in your family has a car, find out the fuel economy figures (miles per gallon) and the size of the fuel tank. Together work out how far the car will go on a full tank of petrol.

If nobody in your family has a car, try to find this information for a car of your choice. You might be able to pick up a brochure from a local car dealer or find the information on the Internet.

Do cars sometimes have more than one fuel economy figure? Why is this? If you have found more than one figure for your car, do a separate calculation for each one.

A BRIDGE TOO FAR

Homework Activity

This map shows the distances in miles between some of the towns close to the River Humber.

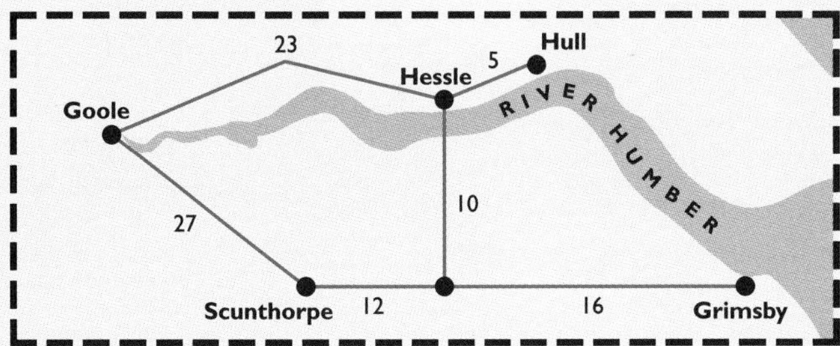

In this activity assume that:

- petrol costs £3 a gallon
- cars travel 45 miles per gallon
- it costs £1.90 to cross the Humber Bridge.

1 Mr Patak lives in Hull and works in Grimsby. How much does it cost him to travel to work (i) via the Humber Bridge? (ii) via Goole and Scunthorpe?

2 Miss Davis lives in Goole and works in Grimsby. How much does it cost her to travel to work (i) via the Humber Bridge? (ii) via Scunthorpe?

3 Mrs McDonald lives in Hull and works in Scunthorpe. How much does it cost her to travel to work (i) via the Humber Bridge? (ii) via Goole?

4 Mr Smith lives in a village on the road between Hull and Goole. He works in Grimsby. It costs exactly the same to travel to work via the Humber Bridge as it does via Goole. Where exactly between Hull and Goole does he live?

~ Ask the family ~

Show the last two questions to someone at home.
Explain your answers to them.
Ask them which route they would take and why.
Make a note of their choices and reasons.

Aim:

~To solve problems involving various measures~

National Curriculum:

~Using and Applying Mathematics 1a, 1b, 2a, 3c, 4a; Number 1b, 4a; Shape, Space and Measures 4c~

Background:

~This activity looks at the sorts of problems facing many motorists all over the country every day. Which is the best route to take and is cost the only factor?~

OLYMPICS '96 - WHO'S THE FASTEST?

Aims:

~To calculate speeds using metric and imperial units~

~To investigate whether people tend to use metric or imperial measures~

National Curriculum:

~Using and Applying Mathematics 1a, 2a; Number 1b, 2a, 4a; Shape, Space and Measures 4a, 4c~

Background:

~We use both metric and imperial measures for distances and speeds. Road signs continue to use miles and we use miles per hour for speed. This activity looks at speeds using both metric and imperial measures. You will need to know that 1 mile is 1.609 kilometres or, put another way, 1 kilometre is 0.62 miles.~

Homework Activity

Here are a few highlights from the 1996 Olympic Games in Atlanta.

- Donovan Bailey of Canada won the gold medal in the men's 100 metres in a world record time of 9.84 seconds.
- Miguel Indurain of Spain won the individual time trial in a time of 1 hour, 4 minutes, 5 seconds. This cycling event was over a distance of 52 kilometres.
- Steve Redgrave and Matthew Pinsent of Great Britain struck gold in the coxless pairs rowing event. Their winning time over the 2 kilometre course was 6 minutes, 20.09 seconds.

For each of these performances use a calculator to work out the speed in

(a) metres per second
(b) kilometres per hour
(c) miles per hour.

Make sure that you make your method clear.

~ Ask the family ~

Pick a few cities, towns or villages which are various distances from your home. Ask people at home if they know how far it is in miles to each of these places. An estimate will do. Then see if they know how far it is in kilometres to each of the places. Do the metric conversion together if necessary.

What conclusions can you make? Do people at home know everyday distances in kilometres, or do they tend to use miles?

BODY RATIOS

Homework Activity - Ask the family

1 Ask someone at home to help you measure your height and armspan accurately in centimetres.

Use a calculator to work out the ratio

$$\frac{\text{height in cm}}{\text{armspan in cm}}$$

Measure the heights and armspans of as many people at home as possible.

Work out their height/armspan ratio.

If someone's ratio is more than 1, what does this mean?

If someone's ratio is less than 1, what does this mean?

Are the ratios roughly the same or do they vary?

Do children have different ratios to adults?

Do males have different ratios to females?

2 Measure the distance from your navel to the floor when you are standing up straight.

Use a calculator to work out the ratio

$$\frac{\text{height of body in cm}}{\text{height of navel in cm}}$$

Work out this ratio for as many people at home as possible and investigate the results.

If someone's ratio is high, what does this mean?

If someone's ratio is low, what does this mean?

If you worked out someone's ratio and found that it was less than 1, what does this mean?

Discuss all of these results with someone at home.

Aims:

~To measure distances accurately~

~To calculate ratios~

~To investigate the ratios of human body measurements~

National Curriculum:

~Using and Applying Mathematics 1a; Number 2b; Shape, Space and Measures 4a~

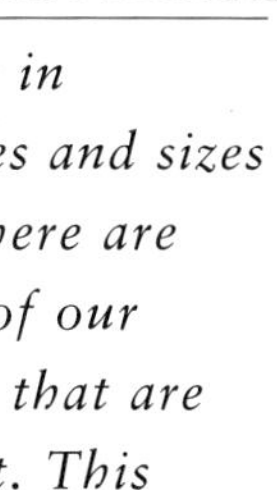

Background:

~We all come in different shapes and sizes but perhaps there are some aspects of our measurements that are fairly constant. This activity investigates the ratios of various body measurements.~

A GOLDEN NUMBER

Aim:

~To explore the properties of an important number in mathematics~

National Curriculum:

~Using and Applying Mathematics 1a, 3a; Number 1b, 4a~

Background:

~Some numbers keep turning up time and time again in very different aspects of mathematics. This activity focuses on one such number.~

Homework Activity

1 Here is a five-pointed star.

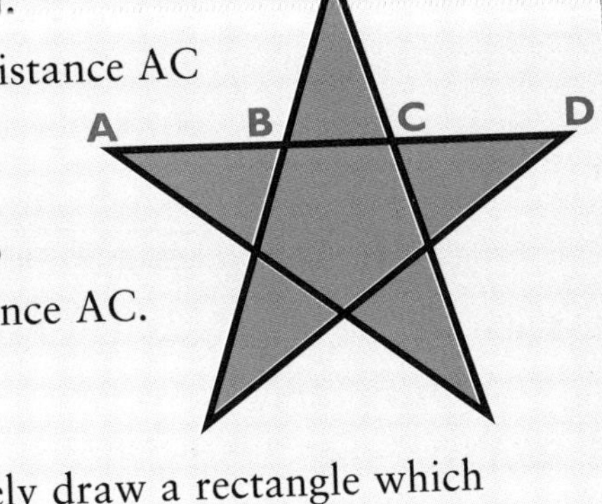

Accurately measure the distance AC and divide it by the distance AB.

Measure the distance AD and divide it by the distance AC.

What do you notice?

2 Accurately draw a rectangle which measures 21 cm by 13 cm. Divide it into a square and a smaller rectangle as shown here. Divide the smaller rectangle into a square and a rectangle.

Repeat this process until you have got five different squares. Write down the length, in centimetres, of each square starting with the smallest. Do the numbers look familiar? Do you know what they are called? Divide the length of the original rectangle by its width. Have you seen the answer before?

3 Use a calculator to work out the value of $\frac{1}{2}(1 + \sqrt{5})$. This number is called the *Golden Ratio*.

~ Ask the family ~

Do this activity with someone at home.

Look around your home and find paintings, photographs, pictures and mirrors that are in rectangular frames.

Measure the length and width of each rectangle.

Divide the length by the width.

Are any of the answers close to the Golden Ratio?

TREASURE HUNT

Homework Activity - Ask the family

Play this game with someone at home.

You might need to explain coordinates to them first.

Mark out a coordinate grid on squared paper like the one shown here. The numbers on your grid should go up to 10 on both axes.

Instructions

Player One picks a point on the grid and writes it down on a piece of paper without showing Player Two.

Player Two must find the point by guessing.

After each guess Player One must tell Player Two how far out he is.

Example: Player One picks the point (3, 2).
Player Two guesses (1, 5).

To get from (1, 5) to (3, 2) you must go down 3 and across 2, a total of 5. So Player One says "You're out by 5".

Player Two then guesses (2, 1).

Player One says "You're out by 2" (i.e. 1 across and 1 up).

Keep a record of the guesses and the other player's responses.

See how many guesses it takes to work out where the point is.

See who can do it in the fewest guesses.

Try to make up a game of your own.

Aim:

~To practise using coordinates~

National Curriculum:

~Using and Applying Mathematics 1a, 2a, 3a, 3b; Shape, Space and Measures 3a~

Background:

~This game for two players provides valuable practice at using coordinates. You will also have to think carefully if you want to beat your opponent.~

PLANE SPOTTING

~To identify symmetry in 3-D objects~

~To produce diagrams which show symmetry in 3-D objects~

~Using and Applying Mathematics 1a, 3a, 3c, 4a; Shape, Space and Measures 1a, 1b, 2a, 2c~

~There are a number of activities in this book which ask you about lines of symmetry in 2-D shapes. A ***plane of symmetry*** *is the 3-D equivalent of a line of symmetry. Think of it as a straight cut which divides the original shape into two symmetrical pieces. This activity asks you to find and sketch planes of symmetry.~*

Homework Activity

1 This box is a cuboid and is 12 cm long, 8 cm wide and 5 cm tall.

Make a sketch, using triangular spotty paper, of the box which shows where one of its planes of symmetry is.

Make further sketches, each one showing a different plane of symmetry.

(Not to scale)

2 Find a container, box or other 3-D object at home which is not a cube or cuboid.

Make a sketch of the object which clearly shows one of its planes of symmetry.

If it has got more than one plane of symmetry, make further sketches to show these.

~ Ask the family ~

Use the cuboid and your own 3-D object to explain planes of symmetry to someone at home.

They might be able to spot planes of symmetry that you have missed. If so, make further sketches to show these.

TRICKY BLOCKS AND BOXES

Homework Activity

1 A box is cube-shaped and has a volume (in cubic centimetres) which is the same as its surface area (in square centimetres).

What size is the cube and what are its volume and surface area?

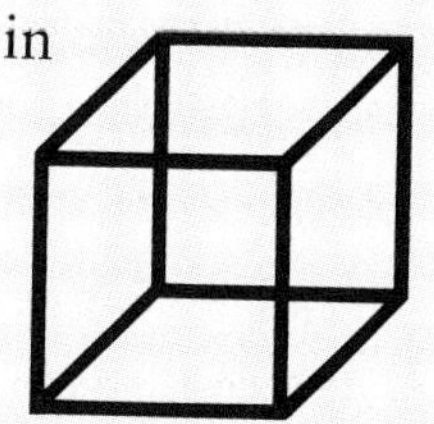

2 Suppose you have a block of wood which is cuboid-shaped. By making two straight cuts with a saw you divide it into three identical cubes. The total surface area of the three cubes is 100 square centimetres more than the surface area of the original block of wood. Work out the volume and surface area of the original block of wood.

~ Ask the family ~

Working with someone at home, find a box whose volume (in cubic centimetres) is more than its surface area (in square centimetres).

Sketch the box and write down its dimensions, its volume and its surface area.

Now find a box whose volume (in cubic centimetres) is less than its surface area (in square centimetres).

Again, sketch the box and write down its dimensions, its volume and its surface area.

If you cannot actually find boxes that fit these descriptions then answer the question by using sketches and calculations.

Aims:

~To solve problems involving volumes and surface areas of 3-D shapes~

~To find and sketch boxes and work out their volumes and surface areas~

National Curriculum:

~Using and Applying Mathematics 1a, 1b, 2a, 2b, 3a, 3c; Shape, Space and Measures 1b, 2a, 4d~

Background:

~You should already know how to work out volumes and surface areas. In this activity you have to use and apply that knowledge to solve two problems and then work out volumes and surface areas of boxes at home.~

FOUR CUBES

Aims:

~*To investigate a shape problem in a logical way*~

~*To think about what we mean by 'the same' and 'different' when we are talking about 3-D shapes*~

National Curriculum:

~*Using and Applying Mathematics 1a, 3c, 4a; Shape, Space and Measures 1b, 2a, 2b*~

Background:

~*This activity asks you to think about 3-D shapes and to make drawings of them. You will also have to think carefully about what is meant by expressions such as 'the same' and 'different' when talking about 3-D shapes.*~

Homework Activity

How many different shapes can you make by clipping together four cubes such as multilink or centicubes?

Make 3-D drawings on spotty paper of all the possible shapes.

Are these two shapes the same or different?

~ Ask the family ~

Show someone at home the two shapes shown above.

Do they think they are the same or different?

Together, decide what you mean by 'the same' and 'different' in this activity.

Write down your definitions of 'the same' and 'different'.

Show them your 3-D drawings.
Do they think any of your shapes are the same?

They might be able to think of some that you have missed out.

WHERE'S IT GONE?

Homework Activity

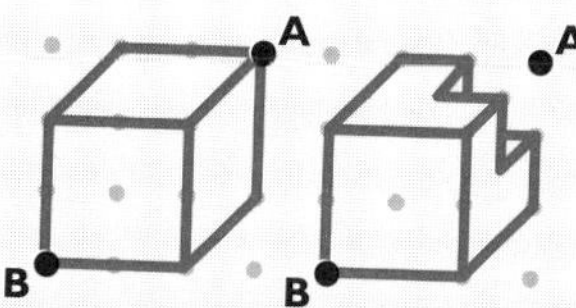

This 3-D drawing on square spotty paper shows a cube with sides of length 2 cm.

The second drawing was made after a cube with sides of length 1 cm had been removed from one of the corners.

Make a 3-D drawing on square spotty paper to show the view from the opposite side.

This drawing shows the same 3-D shape but this time it has been drawn on triangular spotty paper.

A

B

Make a 3-D drawing on triangular spotty paper showing the view from point A looking down towards point B.

~ Ask the family ~

Show this drawing to people at home and ask them what they think it is.

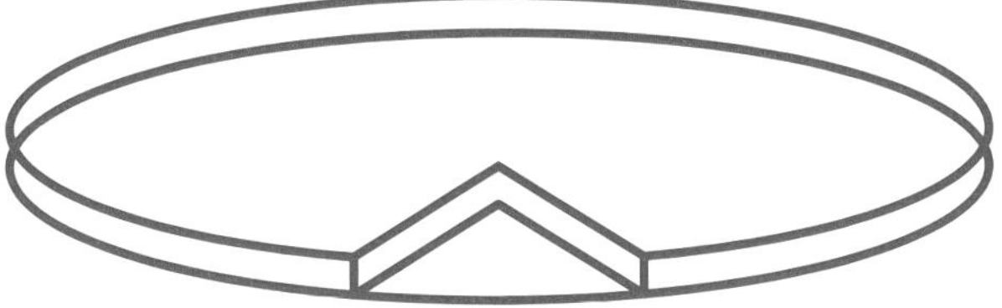

Turn the drawing upside down and ask them what they think it is again.

Let them see your 3-D drawing on triangular spotty paper and ask them what they think it is showing. Turn your drawing upside down and ask them again (your drawing must be correct for the illusion to work).

Aim:

~To practise drawing 3-D objects~

National Curriculum:

~Using and Applying Mathematics 1a, 3c; Shape, Space and Measures 1b, 2a~

Background:

~This activity provides practice at drawing 3-D objects and also shows how these sorts of drawings can sometimes play tricks with your eyes.~

DICEY BUSINESS

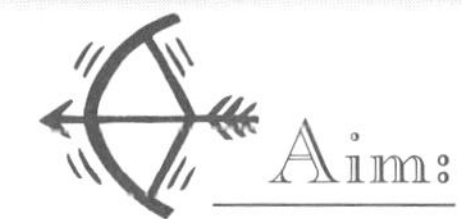

Aim:

~To investigate shape and number by using dice~

National Curriculum:

~Using and Applying Mathematics 1a, 1b, 2a, 3a, 3c, 4a; Algebra 1a, 2b; Shape, Space and Measures 1b, 2a~

Background:

~Have you ever looked closely at the way the numbers are arranged on a dice? If you know the patterns you can impress your friends and family with a clever trick.~

Homework Activity

This flat shape could be cut out, folded and stuck together to make a cube. It is the *net* of a cube.

Draw five different nets of a cube.

Find a six-sided dice.

What do the opposite sides always add up to?

Write the numbers 1 to 6 (or draw spots) on each of your nets so that they would fold together to make a correct dice.

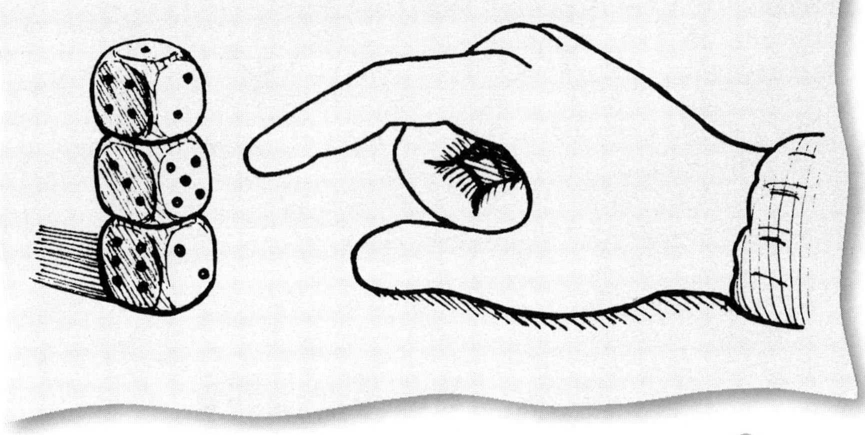

~ Ask the family ~

Try this 'mind-reading' trick with someone at home.

Ask them to stack three dice on top of one another and to add up the numbers on the five hidden faces (the bottom face which is touching the table, plus the faces which are touching one another).

Ask them to call out the number on the top face.

You can quickly tell them the total of the five hidden faces (it is 21 less the number on the top face).

How does the trick work? Try to explain it in your own words.

Homework Activity

This 3-D shape is called an octahedron.

The eight faces are all equilateral triangles.

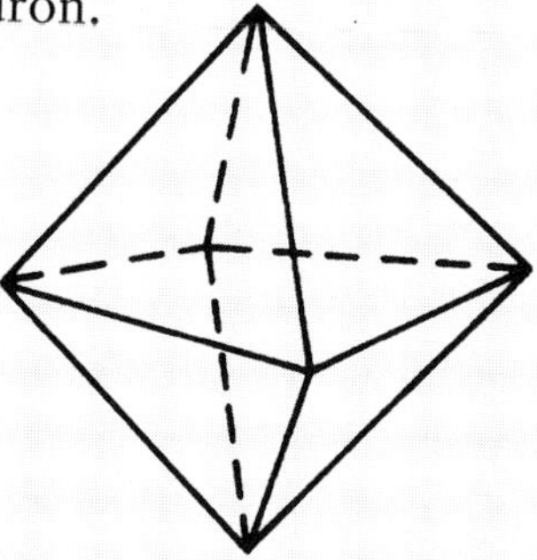

This flat shape could be cut out, folded and stuck together to make an octahedron. It is the *net* of an octahedron.

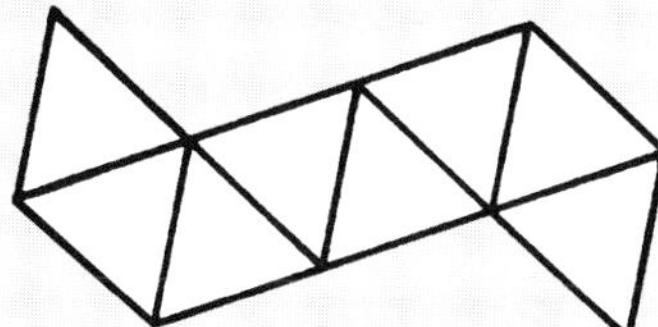

Draw five different nets of an octahedron.

An octahedron can be used as an eight-sided dice.

The numbers on opposite sides must add up to 9.

Write the numbers 1 to 8 on each of your nets so they would fold together to make a correct dice.

~ Ask the family ~

Try this 'mind-reading' trick with someone at home.

Ask them to roll three six-sided dice so you cannot see them (or roll a dice three times and write down the scores, or just pick three numbers from 1 to 6) and then

- double the score on the first dice and add 1
- multiply the answer by 5
- add the score on the second dice
- multiply the answer by 10
- add the score on the third dice

Ask them to tell you the final answer. You must subtract 50 from this to leave a three-figure number whose digits will be the three dice scores.

How does the trick work? Try to explain it in your own words.

Aim:

~To investigate shape and number by using dice~

National Curriculum:

~Using and Applying Mathematics 1a, 1b, 2a, 3a, 3c, 4a; Algebra 1a, 1c, 2b, 3a, 3b, 3c; Shape, Space and Measures 1b, 2a~

Background:

~Most dice that we use are cube-shaped, but there are many other possibilities. This activity investigates the features of an eight-sided dice.~

MAKE A DATE

Aim:

~To spot patterns and solve problems involving dates~

National Curriculum:

~Using and Applying Mathematics 1a, 1b, 2a, 2b; Number 1b; Algebra 2b~

Background:

~Dates are not just for history lessons. There are many dates that are of mathematical interest as you will soon discover. Work on these problems with someone at home.~

Homework Activity - Ask the family

1 What is special about the 6th July 1989? (Hint: Write it as 6/7/89 and look at the pattern in the numbers.) When were the last three dates that patterns like this occurred? When are the next three dates that it will occur?

2 What is special about the 19th March 1991? (Hint: Find out about palindromes on page 15.) When were the last three dates that this occurred? When are the next three dates that it will occur?

3 What is special about the 14th July 1998? (Hint: Write it as 14/7/98 and multiply the day and the month.) When were the last three dates that this occurred? When are the next three dates that it will occur? Explain why there are no dates like this in 1997.

4 What is special about the 12th August 1920? (Hint: Write it as 12/8/20 and add the day and month.) When were the last three dates that this occurred? When are the next three dates that it will occur?

5 What is the maximum number of Friday 13ths you can have in one year? When was the last time this happened?

6 Christmas Day this year will not be on the same day of the week as it was last year. How many years will we have to wait for every day of the year to be on the same day of the week as this year?

FIND THE FRACTION

Homework Activity - Ask the family

1 Everyone knows that 0.5 = $^1/_2$ and 0.25 = $^1/_4$ but what about these?
Use a calçulator to find the fraction that is equivalent to these decimals (most of the numerators and denominators are single-figure numbers).

(i) 0.7777777 (ii) 0.8333333 (iii) 0.4166666

(iv) 0.7333333 (v) 0.4285714

Briefly explain in your own words how you tackled these questions.

2 Write down the next three fractions in this sequence: $^1/_2$, $^1/_4$, $^1/_8$, $^1/_{16}$.
If the sequence was continued and all the fractions added together what would the total be? Give reasons for your answer.

3 Write down the next three fractions in this sequence: $^1/_3$, $^1/_9$, $^1/_{27}$.
What would the total of all the fractions in this sequence be? Give reasons for your answer.

4 A farmer died and in his will asked that his 17 horses be shared out as follows:

- half of them to be given to his wife
- one-third of them to be given to his son
- one-ninth of them to be given to his daughter.

The family were completely baffled but the solicitor in charge was able to sort it out – but how?

(Turn to the bottom of page 76 if you would like a clue.)

Aim:

~To solve various problems involving fractions~

National Curriculum:

~Using and Applying Mathematics 1a, 1b, 2a, 4a; Number 1a, 2b; Algebra 2b~

Background:

~Here are a few problems, puzzles and investigative activities on the theme of fractions. Try to solve them with the help of someone at home.~

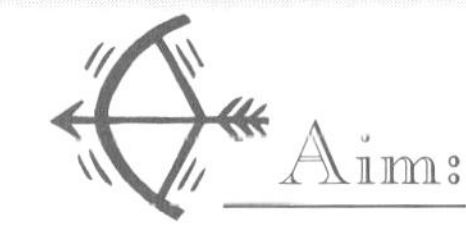

Aim:

~To investigate patterns in calendars and other number grids~

National Curriculum:

~Using and Applying Mathematics 1a, 1b, 2a, 4a, 4b, 4c; Number 1b; Algebra 1a, 2b~

Homework Activity

1 Pick any 2 by 2 block of numbers on a calendar like the one shown here.

Multiply together the numbers in diagonally opposite corners (e.g. 9 x 17 and 10 x 16).

Work out the difference between the two answers.

Do the same with other 2 by 2 blocks of numbers.

What do you notice?

2 Pick any 3 by 3 block of numbers.

Again, multiply together the numbers in diagonally opposite corners and work out the difference between the two answers.

Try it for several different 3 by 3 blocks.

What do you notice?

The farmer's horses

The solicitor brought along an extra horse. Now try working out the fractions using 18 horses instead of 17.

Background:

~Calendars contain many interesting number patterns. If you know about these patterns you can impress your friends and family with a few clever tricks.~

~ Ask the family ~

Try these 'mind-reading' tricks with someone at home.

1 Give someone a calendar set out like the one shown opposite and ask them to pick a 2 by 2 block of numbers. Ask them to call out the smallest number. You can immediately tell them the biggest (8 more than the smallest) and the total (multiply the smallest by 4 and add 16).

2 Ask them to pick a 3 by 3 block and call out the smallest number. You can tell them the biggest (16 more than the smallest) and the total (multiply the smallest by 9 and add 72).

How do these tricks work?
Try to explain them in your own words.

Suppose you used a 100-square instead of a calendar and asked the other person to pick a 2 by 2 block of numbers and call out the smallest one. Would you be able to work out the biggest number and the total?

What about a 3 by 3 block?

MINI-LOTTERY

Aims:

~To work in a methodical and logical way~

~To spot patterns and relationships~

National Curriculum:

~Using and Applying Mathematics 1a, 1b, 2a, 2b, 4a; Algebra 1a, 1c, 2b~

Background:

~We all know about the National Lottery but do we know about the mathematics that is involved? This activity starts with a simplified lottery and works through a series of stages that gradually get more complex. By the end you should be starting to realise that the number of possible combinations in the National Lottery is very large.~

Homework Activity

The UK National Lottery is based on picking six balls from 49 balls, numbered 1 to 49.

Suppose there was a Mini-Lottery in which two balls were picked from five balls, numbered 1 to 5.

One possible Mini-Lottery result is shown below.

List all the possible Mini-Lottery results there could be.

What if two balls were picked from six balls, numbered 1 to 6?

How many possible Mini-Lottery results would there be now?

List them all.

What about two balls picked from seven balls, numbered 1 to 7?

What about two balls picked from eight balls, numbered 1 to 8?

Can you spot any patterns or quick ways of working out how many possible results there are each time?

~ Ask the family ~

Explain to someone at home exactly what you have been doing. Show them how you have been working out the number of possible Mini-Lottery results each time.

Work together to see if you can find how many possible Mini-Lottery results there would be if we were picking two balls from 49, numbered 1 to 49.

COUNTING SHEEP

Homework Activity - Ask the family

A farm consisted of a large square piece of land which was divided into nine smaller square fields. The farmhouse, in the middle field, had a large window along each outside wall. The farmer could see three fields when he looked out of each window. For example, when he looked out of the north window he could see fields A, B and C.

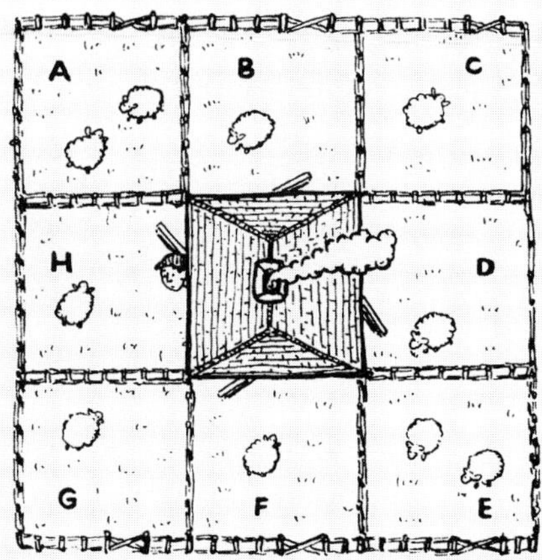

The farmer had ten sheep. He asked his son to arrange the sheep in the eight fields so that he would always be able to see four sheep when he looked out of each window.

The diagram shows how he did it.

Check that four sheep can be seen from each window.

Can you arrange the sheep so that you can see five sheep from each window?

What about six sheep? What about three sheep?

Make sketches to show the ones that are possible.

Suppose the farmer had eleven sheep. Is it possible to arrange the sheep so that the farmer can see two sheep, three sheep, four sheep, ... out of each window?

Make sketches to show the ones that are possible.

Suppose the farmer had thirteen or fourteen sheep. What are the possibilities now?

Aim:

~To work in an investigative way on problems involving pattern~

National Curriculum:

~Using and Applying Mathematics 1a, 1b, 2a, 2b, 3c, 4a, 4b, 4c, 4d, 4e; Algebra 1a, 2b~

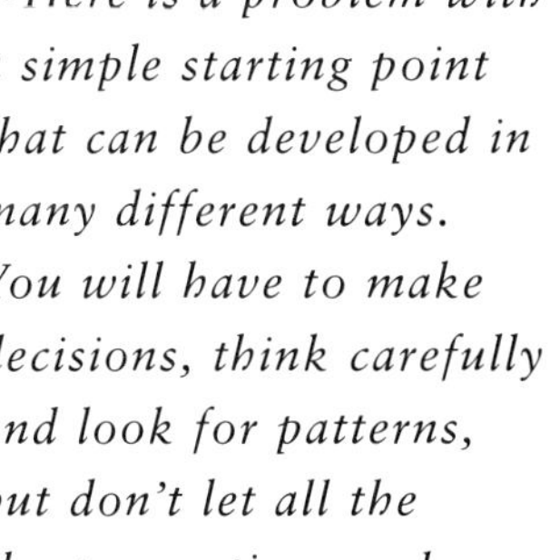

Background:

~Here is a problem with a simple starting point that can be developed in many different ways. You will have to make decisions, think carefully and look for patterns, but don't let all the sheep-counting send you to sleep! Work on it with someone at home.~

NEIGHBOURS

Aim:

~To investigate patterns and relationships in consecutive numbers~

National Curriculum:

~Using and Applying Mathematics 1a, 1b, 2a, 4a, 4b, 4c; Number 1b; Algebra 1a, 2b, 3a, 3b, 3c~

Background:

~Here is another opportunity to impress your friends and family with your mind-reading. But can you spot how it works?~

Homework Activity

Add together any three consecutive numbers, for example 8, 9 and 10. Choose another three consecutive numbers and add them together. Repeat this several times. Is there a connection between the middle number and the total?

12 can be made by adding three consecutive numbers. What are the numbers? Can 20 be made in this way?

Which numbers can be made in this way?

Which numbers can be made by adding two consecutive numbers? Which numbers can be made by adding four consecutive numbers?

Are there any numbers less than 100 which cannot be made by adding consecutive numbers? If so, work them out.

~ Ask the family ~

Try this 'mind-reading' trick with someone at home.

Ask them to pick three consecutive numbers no bigger than 50.

Then ask them to call out any multiple of 3 less than 100.

They must add these four numbers together and multiply the answer by 67 (let them use a calculator).

Ask them to call out the last two digits of the answer.

You should be able to work out the missing digits in the answer and also the three consecutive numbers like this:

- Divide the multiple of 3 by 3 and add 1.
- Subtract this from the two-digit number they call out.
- This gives the first of the three consecutive numbers (so you can quickly work out the other two).
- To get the missing digits, simply double the two-digit number they call out.

SQUARE ROOT AND MULTIPLY

Homework Activity

Use a calculator to work through this cycle of key-presses.

You can start with any number you want but must keep going round until the number you get at the end of each cycle seems to be about the same each time.

What number do you end up with?

Try a completely different starting number.

Does it make a difference?

Instead of multiplying by 2 try multiplying by 3.

What number do you end up with this time?

What if you multiply by 4 each time?

What if you multiply by 5 each time?

What if you multiply by 6 each time?

Can you spot any patterns in your results?

Explain these carefully.

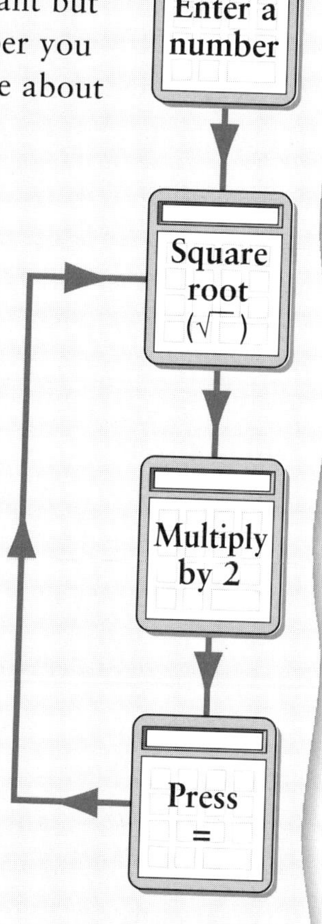

~ Ask the family ~

Show someone at home what you have been doing.

Let them choose the starting number and the number you multiply by each time and then you predict the number you will end up with.

Aims:

~To follow a set of instructions~

~To spot patterns and relationships~

~To use the patterns and relationships to make predictions~

National Curriculum:

~Using and Applying Mathematics 1a, 1b, 4a, 4b, 4c; Number 1a, 3e; Algebra 1a, 2b~

Background:

~Calculators are very good at finding square roots and multiplying decimals, but there are some things that a calculator cannot do. In this activity you can let the calculator do the arithmetic but you must try to spot patterns and relationships in the numbers.~

DIVIDE AND ADD

Aims:

~ *To follow a set of instructions* ~

~ *To spot patterns and relationships* ~

~ *To use the patterns and relationships to make predictions* ~

National Curriculum:

~ *Using and Applying Mathematics 1a, 1b, 4a, 4b, 4c; Number 1a, 3e; Algebra 1a, 2b* ~

Background:

~ *Calculators are very good at doing arithmetic as long as you press the right keys! But there are some things that a calculator cannot do, for example spot patterns or relationships. Let the calculator do the arithmetic in this activity while you concentrate on harder things.* ~

Homework Activity

Use a calculator to work through this cycle of key-presses.

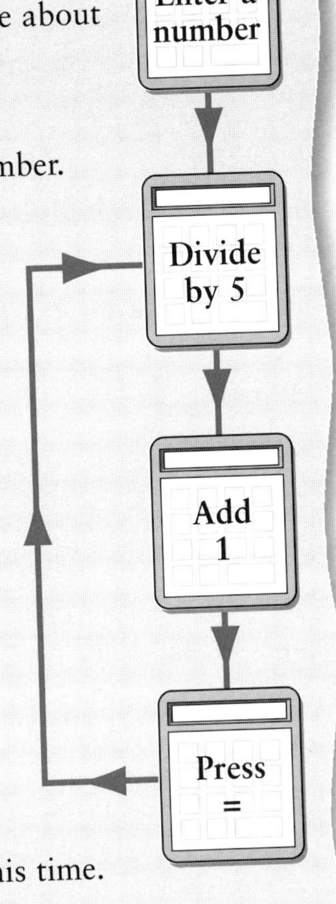

You can start with any number you want but must keep going round until the number you get at the end of each cycle seems to be about the same each time.

What number do you end up with?

Try a completely different starting number.

Try starting with a negative number.

Does it make a difference?

Instead of adding 1 try adding 2 each time. What number do you end up with this time?

What if you add 3 each time?

What if you subtract 1 each time?

What if you subtract 2 each time?

Can you spot any patterns in your results?

Explain these carefully.

Try all of these again but this time divide by 4 instead of by 5.

Explain any patterns you can spot this time.

~ Ask the family ~

Show someone at home what you have been doing.

You could let them choose the starting number, the number you divide by and the number you add or subtract each time and then you predict the number you will end up with.

DIVIDE AND ADD AGAIN

Homework Activity

In the *Divide and Add* activity you only divided by whole numbers such as 5 and 4. This time you must try dividing by other types of numbers. Use a calculator to work through this cycle of key-presses. Remember, you can start with any number you want and you must keep going round the cycle of key-presses until the number you get after pressing the equals key seems to be about the same each time.

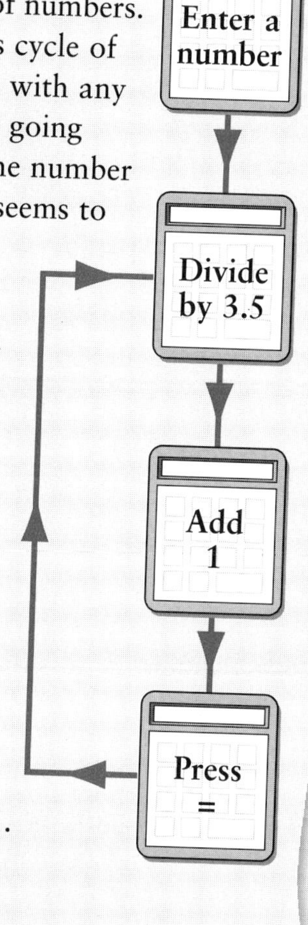

What number do you end up with?
Try dividing by 2.5. What do you end up with this time? What if you divide by 1.5? Try dividing by other decimal numbers greater than 1. Can you spot any patterns or relationships in your results?

Go back and remind yourself of the patterns and relationships in *Divide and Add.*

Are these relationships still true when we divide by decimal numbers?

Try dividing by any number less than 1.

What do you notice?

Try to explain why this happens.

~ Ask the family ~

Show the cycle of key-presses shown above to someone at home. Let them choose the starting number and the number you divide by and then you predict the number you will end up with.

Aims:

~To follow a set of instructions~

~To spot patterns and relationships~

~To use the patterns and relationships to make predictions~

National Curriculum:

~Using and Applying Mathematics 1a, 1b, 4a, 4b, 4c; Number 1a, 3e; Algebra 1a, 2b~

Background:

*~You must do the **Divide and Add** activity on page 82 before attempting this one. Like the earlier activity, this one is concerned with patterns and relationships in numbers produced by a calculator.~*

THINK OF A NUMBER

Aims:

~To understand that addition and subtraction are the inverse of one another~

~To understand that multiplication and division are the inverse of one another~

~To practise mental arithmetic skills~

National Curriculum:

~Using and Applying Mathematics 1a, 2a; Number 1b, 4a; Algebra 1a, 1b~

Background:

~Activities like this have been popular for decades, but are you aware of the mathematics that is involved? Do this activity with someone at home.~

Homework Activity - Ask the family

When they have told you their answer, you must work out in your head what their starting number was.

Check with the other person to see if you were right.

Try it again and see if you can work out the starting number quicker this time.

Try using these instructions:

- Multiply their number by 3 and then subtract 5.
- Halve their number and then add 1.
- Add 5 to their number and then double the answer.

You might also like to try instructions of your own.

Remember, the other person tells you their final answer each time and then you must work out their starting number.

Afterwards, write down an explanation of how you worked out the starting number for each set of instructions.

THINK OF ANOTHER NUMBER

Homework Activity

Go back to page 84 and read about the *Think of a Number* activity. If we let the starting number be shown by the letter x then we can use the instructions and the final answer to make an equation, like this.

The *Think of a Number* activity on page 84 uses four sets of instructions. Suppose the final answers for the four sets of instructions are 21, 13, 5 and 32. Write down an equation for each set of instructions and solve it to find the starting number each time.

Suppose you used all four sets of instructions with someone, and their final answer was 31 every time. Write down four equations and solve them to find the four starting numbers.

~ Ask the family ~

Make up a set of instructions and try using them with someone at home. Get them to tell you their final answer, write down the equation and then solve it to find the starting number.

Try doing this with a few different sets of instructions.

Aims:

~To turn a set of instructions into an algebraic expression~

~To solve a simple equation~

National Curriculum:

~Using and Applying Mathematics 1a, 3a; Algebra 1a, 1c, 3a, 3b, 3c, 3d~

Background:

~Sometimes we can use algebra to help us solve everyday puzzles and problems. This activity asks you to turn a ***Think of a Number*** *activity into an equation and then solve it.~*

Aims:

~To use algebra to explain why a number trick works~

~To make algebraic expressions~

National Curriculum:

~Using and Applying Mathematics 1a, 3a; Algebra 1a, 1c, 3a, 3b, 3c~

Background:

~An opportunity to impress other people with your number wizardry, but can you explain what is going on by using your knowledge of algebra?~

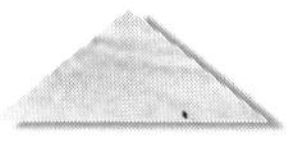

Homework Activity - Ask the family

Try this with a few different people at home. Remember, if you use these instructions the other person's answer will always be 3.

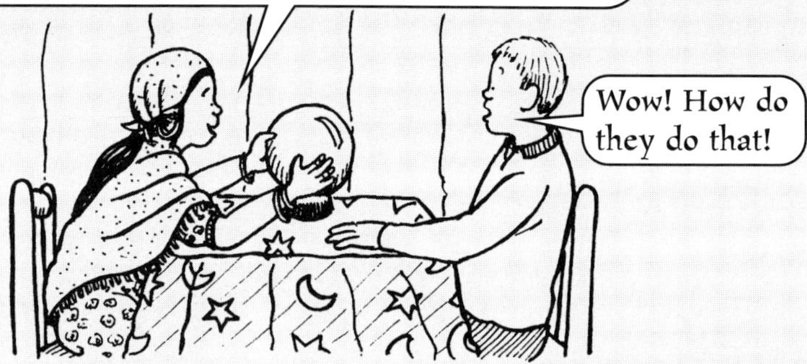

Can you explain why the final answer is always 3?

Let x stand for the starting number. Make an algebraic expression for the answer after each step of the instructions. What do you end up with after following all of the instructions?

If you had asked the other person to add 10 instead of 6, what would their final answer always be? Try it with people at home and see if it works.

If you had asked them to add 5 instead of 6, what would their final answer always be? Again, try it with people at home and see if it works.

Make up a set of instructions of your own which will always produce the same final answer no matter what the starting number is. Try it out with people at home to make sure it works. Use algebra to explain why.

LEONARDO OF PISA

Homework Activity

This sequence is called the *Fibonacci sequence*, named after the Italian mathematician Leonardo of Pisa who was better known as Fibonacci.

1, 1, 2, 3, 5, 8, 13, 21, ...

1 Can you spot the pattern in the Fibonacci sequence? Write down the numbers above followed by the next seven in the sequence.

2 Pick out the numbers which are multiples of 3. What do you notice?

3 Pick any number and divide it by the previous number using a calculator. Do this for the last five numbers in your sequence. What do you notice?

4 Make up your own adding sequence by choosing any two starting numbers. e.g. 4, 9, 13, 22, ... Write down the first fifteen numbers in your sequence. Do 2 and 3 again, but this time for your own sequence.

What do you find this time?

Aim:

~To investigate patterns and relationships in number sequences~

National Curriculum:

~Using and Applying Mathematics 1a, 1b, 3a, 4a, 4b, 4c; Number 1b; Algebra 1a, 2b~

Background:

~The Fibonacci sequence is discussed in the ***Miles, Kilometres and Fibonacci*** *activity on page 56 but in this activity you have to investigate it in more detail.~*

~ Ask the family ~

Show someone at home how to make adding sequences like Fibonacci. Ask them to write down two numbers that add up to 10 and use these as the first two numbers in an adding sequence. Keep going until there are eight numbers altogether.

Ask them to tell you what the last number in the sequence is.

You can tell them one of the first two numbers by subtracting 80 from the last number and dividing the answer by 5. You can work out the other because they add up to 10.

How does the trick work? Try to explain it in your own words.

HOW HOT?

Aims:

~To convert temperatures from Celsius to Fahrenheit~

~To compare two slightly different ways of converting~

National Curriculum:

~Using and Applying Mathematics 1a, 4a; Number 1b, 2b, 4a, 4b; Algebra 1a, 3b~

Background:

~Many people think of temperatures in terms of Fahrenheit rather than Celsius. This activity compares two ways of converting from one to the other.~

Homework Activity

Here is a rough way of converting Celsius temperatures to Fahrenheit.

Fahrenheit = 2 × Celsius + 30

Use this rough conversion to change these to Fahrenheit.

(a) 0° C (freezing point)
(b) 100° C (boiling point)
(c) 25° C (a warm summer day in the UK)
(d) 40° C (a hot summer day in North Africa)
(e) -5° C (a cold winter day in the UK)

A more accurate conversion is Fahrenheit = $\frac{9 \times \text{Celsius}}{5} + 32$

Use the accurate conversion to change the Celsius temperatures to Fahrenheit.

Do you think the rough conversion is good enough for everyday temperatures?

Give reasons for your answer.

Explain in your own words how you would convert 60° F to Celsius.

~ Ask the family ~

Ask people at home if they prefer to use temperatures in Celsius or in Fahrenheit and ask them to explain why. Try to ask as many people as you can.

Show the five Celsius temperatures above to people at home and ask them if they know roughly what they are in Fahrenheit.

Do they know how to convert from Celsius to Fahrenheit?

Explain to them the two conversions you have used in this activity.

Together, find the temperature which is the same in Celsius as it is in Fahrenheit.

FIRST TO 100

Homework Activity - Ask the family

Game 1: Player One calls out a number from 1 to 5. Player Two adds a number from 1 to 5 and calls out the total. Player One adds a number from 1 to 5 and calls out the new total. Keep going like this. The winner is the person who calls out 31.

Game 2: Same as Game 1 but this time you can call out numbers from 1 to 10 and the winner is the first person to call out 100.

Game 3: Make two piles of matches, counters, coins or scraps of paper. The two piles do not have to be equal. Players take it in turn to remove objects from the piles. You can *either* take any number of objects from one pile *or* take an equal number from both piles (e.g. 3 from each). The winner is the person who picks up the last object.

Play each game a few times so that you understand what is going on. Then go away and try to work out a winning strategy. Try working backwards from the winning move to the starting position. When you think you know how to win, play again with someone at home.

Explain your winning strategies in your own words.

Aims:

~To practise mental arithmetic by playing number games~

~To investigate winning strategies for these games~

National Curriculum:

~Using and Applying Mathematics 1a, 1b, 2a, 2b, 4a, 4b, 4c, 4d; Number 1b; Algebra 2b~

Background:

~Here are three number games for two people. Don't rely on luck. Try to work out a winning strategy so that you can always beat your opponent.~

PRIME TIME

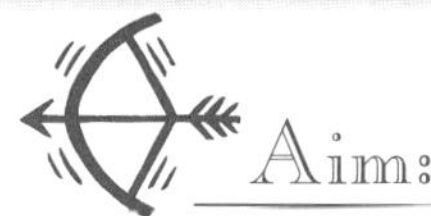

Aim:

~To investigate some of the properties of prime numbers~

National Curriculum:

~Using and Applying Mathematics 1a, 1b, 2a, 3a; Number 1b, 3a, 4b; Algebra 2a, 2b, 3b~

Background:

~You should already know what a prime number is (a number which is divisible ***only*** *by itself and 1). In this activity you will explore some of their properties that are not so widely known.~*

Homework Activity

(a) On a 100-square shade all of the multiples of 6. In a different colour shade all of the prime numbers. What do you notice?

(b) By substituting the numbers 1 to 9 in place of n in $n^2 + n + 11$ you can generate prime numbers.

For example if $n = 1$, you get $(1)^2 + (1) + 11 = 13$.

Use values of n from 2 to 9 to generate other prime numbers.

(c) You can also generate prime numbers with $n^2 - n + 41$ for values of n from 1 to 40. Choose values of n which generate prime numbers less than 100.

(d) The expression $\sqrt{1 + 24n}$ will generate every prime number except 2 and 3, although not every value of n produces a prime number. For example if $n = 2$, you get $\sqrt{1 + 24(2)} = \sqrt{49} = 7$ which is prime.

But if $n = 3$, you get $\sqrt{1 + 24(3)} = \sqrt{73} = 8.544$.

Find the values of n which generate prime numbers less than 20.

~ Ask the family ~

Try this 'mind-reading' trick with someone at home.

Ask them to choose any prime number greater than 3 (or you could show them your shaded primes on the 100-square).

They must square the prime number, add 17, divide the answer by 12 and work out the remainder. The remainder will always be 6, so surprise them by telling them. Alternatively, ask them to make further calculations, for example: "Double the remainder and add 3. Your answer is 15."

PROVE IT!

Homework Activity

Decide whether each of the four statements below is true or false. You must use examples to support your answers, or you might be able to prove whether they are true or false by using algebra.

1 You have a square and a rectangle. The length of the rectangle is 1 centimetre more than the length of the square. The width of the rectangle is 1 centimetre less than the width of the square. The square and the rectangle will always have the same perimeter.

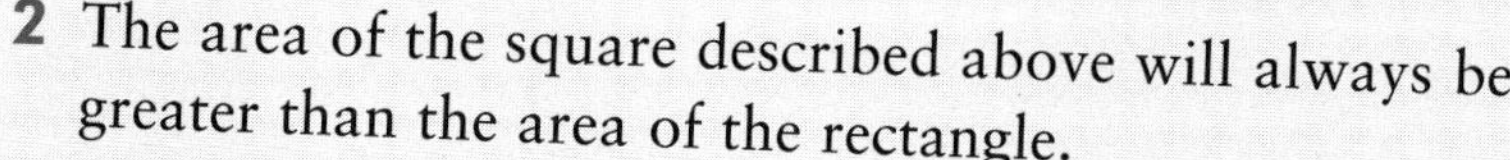

2 The area of the square described above will always be greater than the area of the rectangle.

3 You have a cube and a cuboid. The length of the cuboid is 1 centimetre more than the length of the cube. The width of the cuboid is the same as the width of the cube. The height of the cuboid is 1 centimetre less than the height of the cube. The volume of the cube will always be greater than the volume of the cuboid.

4 The surface area of the cube described above will always be greater than the surface area of the cuboid.

~ Ask the family ~

Show the four statements to someone at home and explain whether they are true or false. Use sketches of squares, rectangles, cubes and cuboids to help your explanations.

Aims:

~To show an understanding of perimeter, area, surface area and volume~

~To prove statements using examples or by using algebra~

National Curriculum:

~Using and Applying Mathematics 1a, 1b, 1c, 2a, 3a, 3c, 4a, 4b, 4c, 4d, 4e; Algebra 1a, 1c, 3a, 3b, 3c; Shape, Space and Measures 4d~

Background:

~You should have already had lots of practice at working out perimeters, areas, surface areas and volumes. This activity is not so straightforward. You must find your own way of showing whether each of these four statements is true or false.~

MISLEADING GRAPHS

Aims:

~To identify how graphs can be misleading~

~To interpret information presented on a graph~

National Curriculum:

~Using and Applying Mathematics 1a, 3b, 3d; Algebra 2c; Handling Data 1e, 2f~

Background:

~We are constantly bombarded with graphs and statistics in newspapers, magazines and on television. These must be read with care because they can sometimes be misleading.~

Homework Activity

Look at this graph and quickly decide whether the Sales Manager is right or not.

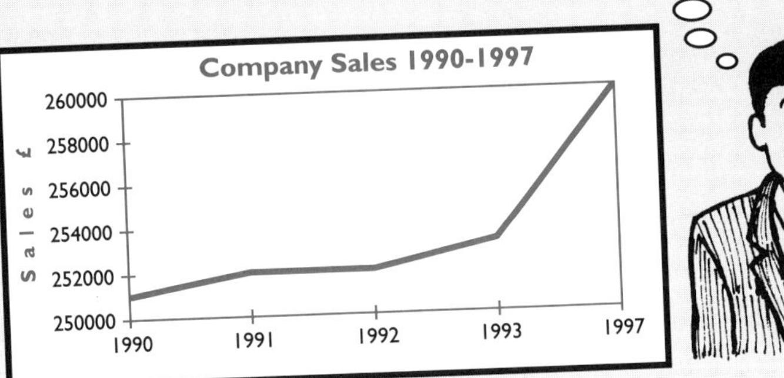

Answer the following questions.

1 By how much did sales rise
(a) between 1990 and 1993? (b) between 1993 and 1997?

2 On average, by how much per year did sales rise
(a) between 1990 and 1993? (b) between 1993 and 1997?

3 Is the Sales Manager right? Give reasons for your answer.

4 Explain how the graph could mislead people.
How could it be improved?

~ Ask the family ~

Show the graph to someone at home and ask them if they think the Sales Manager is right or wrong. If they are misled by the graph you might have to explain it to them.

Together, try to find a graph in a newspaper or magazine that could be misleading. Cut it out or make a copy of it and talk about why it could be misleading.

A PIECE OF CAKE?

Homework Activity

These pie charts show the proportion of pupils getting grades A, B, C and D in the Y7 and Y8 maths exam.

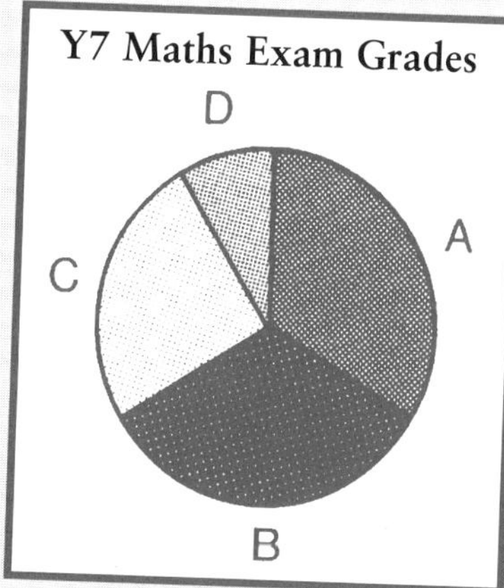

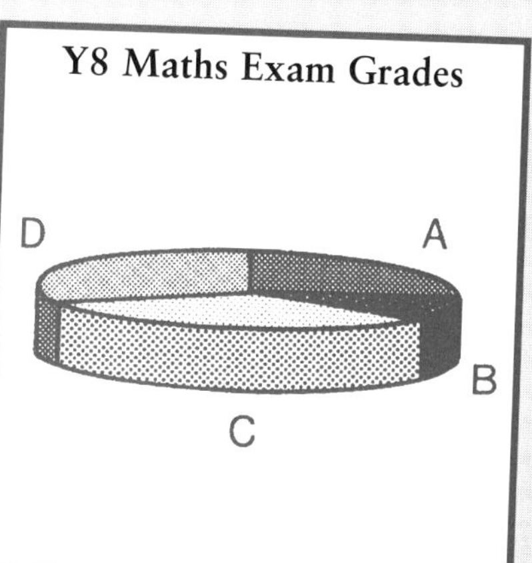

Estimate the percentage of pupils in Y7 and in Y8 who were awarded each grade.
Write down your estimates.

~ Ask the family ~

Ask someone at home to estimate the percentage of pupils in Y7 and Y8 who were awarded each grade. Write down their estimates.

Now turn to the bottom of page 94 where you will find the actual percentages. Compare these with your estimates.

Were your estimates better for the Y7 chart or for the Y8 chart? Why do you think this is?

Find examples of 3-D graphs and charts in newspapers and magazines and bring them in to school.

Aims:

~To estimate figures shown on pie charts~

~To think about the limitations of some 3-D charts~

National Curriculum:

~Using and Applying Mathematics 1a, 3b, 3d; Handling Data 1e, 2f~

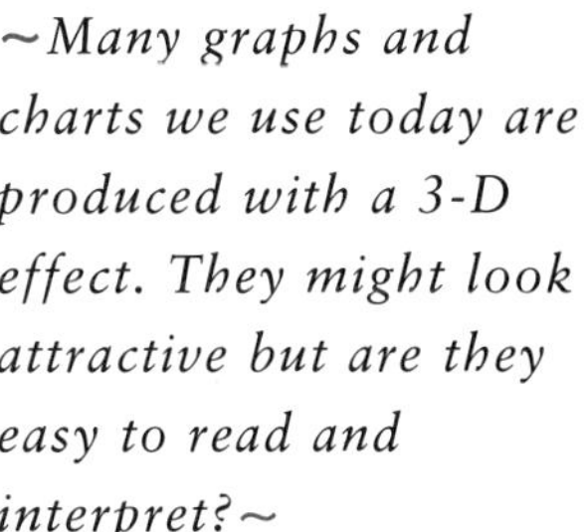

Background:

~Many graphs and charts we use today are produced with a 3-D effect. They might look attractive but are they easy to read and interpret?~

A GOOD READ?

Aim:

~To plan and carry out a data handling activity~

National Curriculum:

~Using and Applying Mathematics 1a, 1b, 2a, 2b, 2c, 3c, 4a, 4b, 4c; Handling Data 1b, 2c, 2d, 2e, 2f~

Background:

~A good author or journalist will write in a style that is suitable for the intended audience. Books for young children are written in a very different style from novels for adults. In this activity you should work with someone at home to investigate different styles of writing.~

Homework Activity - Ask the family

Find *either* a children's book and a book aimed at adults, *or* two different types of newspaper.

By carefully analysing the two books or two newspapers, decide whether or not they are written in different styles.

Start by discussing how you are going to carry out the analysis.

You might like to think about questions such as:

- How can we compare the two writing styles?
- What information do we need to gather?
- What will we do with the information?
- How can we present it so that other people can make sense of it?

Write a report which explains how you tackled the investigation and what you discovered. Include all of the things you found out about the two books or newspapers and show any calculations that you made. You can use a calculator but your method must be clear to someone reading the report.

Homework information for page 93

Exam grades: Y7 A 33%, B 33%, C 25%, D 9%

Y8 A 25%, B 9%, C 33%, D 33%

DEALS ON WHEELS

Homework Activity - Ask the family

Are second-hand cars sold by car dealers more expensive than those sold by private individuals?

Discuss this question with someone at home and work together to plan how you are going to answer it.

You might need to think about questions such as:

- What makes and models of cars shall we look at?
- What ages of car shall we look at?
- Where can we find the information?
- How much information do we need?
- What are we going to do with the information?
- How are we going to compare the prices?
- How are we going to present the findings?

Write a report which explains how you tackled the problem and what you discovered. Include all of the useful information you gathered and show any calculations that you made. You can use a calculator but your method must be clear to someone reading the report.

Aim:

~To plan and carry out a data handling activity~

National Curriculum:

~Using and Applying Mathematics 1a, 1b, 2a, 2b, 2c, 3c, 4a, 4b, 4c; Handling Data 1b, 2a, 2c, 2d, 2f~

Background:

~Many of us will buy a car at some time during our lives. This activity asks you to work with someone at home to investigate one important aspect of car buying.~

HOME AND AWAY

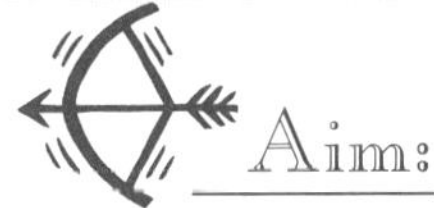

Aim:

~To plan and carry out a data handling activity~

National Curriculum:

~Using and Applying Mathematics 1a, 1b, 2a, 2b, 2c, 3c, 4a, 4b, 4c; Handling Data 1b, 2a, 2c, 2d, 2e, 2f~

Background:

~We tend to think that football teams do better at home than they do away, but is there any hard evidence to support this? In this activity you should work with someone at home to look for the evidence and present it.~

Homework Activity - Ask the family

Is it true that football teams perform better when they are playing at home than they do when they are playing away?

Talk about this with someone at home. They might be able to make useful suggestions when you are planning how to tackle it and also help you to actually carry out the investigation.

You might need to talk about things such as:

- Which teams, leagues or divisions are we going to use?
- How many matches should we look at?
- How can we compare the home and away performances?
- Where can we find the information?
- What are we going to do with the information?
- How are we going to present the findings?
- What do our findings show?

Write a report which explains how you tackled the problem and what you discovered. Include all of the useful information you gathered and show any calculations that you made. You can use a calculator but your method must be clear to someone reading the report.

FAT CHANCE

Homework Activity - Ask the family

Here are twelve events. Write each one on a separate piece of paper.

1 England win the next football World Cup.

2 It rains here tomorrow.

3 You get a head when you flick a 10p piece.

4 Your maths teacher comes to school tomorrow.

5 You get a six when you roll a normal six-sided dice.

6 England win their next football match.

7 You will grow to be 20 feet tall.

8 All of the Smarties in a tube will be the same colour.

9 You get a three when you roll a normal six-sided dice.

10 It will rain somewhere in the world today.

11 The next Pope will be a man.

12 The sun will not be shining here at midnight tonight.

Arrange the twelve events into three piles:

- an 'impossible' pile
- a 'might happen' pile
- a 'certain' pile

Make a note of which events are in each pile. Did you both agree on where each event belongs? Make a note of any you did not agree on.

Now arrange the events in the 'might happen' pile in order. Some will be close to 'impossible', some will be close to 'certain' and some will be roughly in the middle.

Make a note of your final order. Did you both agree on the order? Make a note of the things you did not agree on.

Aim:

~To arrange events in order according to how likely it is that they will occur~

National Curriculum:

~Using and Applying Mathematics 1a, 3a, 4a; Handling Data 1d, 3a~

Background:

~Very few things in life are certain. In this activity you have to think about things that are certain, are impossible or might happen. Do this activity with someone at home. It should result in a lot of important discussion.~

WE ALL HAVE OUR UPS AND DOWNS

Aims:

~To think about what is meant by 'fair' in probability work~

~To decide whether or not a probability game is fair~

National Curriculum:

~Using and Applying Mathematics 1a, 3a, 3b, 4a; Handling Data 1d, 3a, 3c~

Background:

~Rarely are we certain of the way something is going to turn out, for example in raffles, lotteries and other games of chance. We often think "It's not fair", but what do we mean by 'fair'?~

Homework Activity - Ask the family

Suppose you were playing a game in which you could either win or lose, or a game for two players in which one player would be the winner. What do we mean if we say that it is "a fair game"? Discuss this with someone at home and see what they think. Write down what you mean by "a fair game".

Play and talk about this game with someone at home. You are playing together, not against one another.

Instructions

- Place a counter on the START.

  Flick a coin.

  HEADS - move up one space.

  TAILS - move up two spaces.

  If you land on a shaded space, follow the arrows.

  Keep flicking and moving until you WIN or LOSE.

  Play lots of times and keep a record of the results.

  Is it a fair game? Give reasons for your answer.

- Suppose it costs 5p to play the game.

  WIN you get 20p.

  LOSE you get nothing. Is it worth playing the game?

  Give reasons for your answer.

- It is impossible to land on one of the spaces. Which one?

WE ALL HAVE OUR UPS AND DOWNS

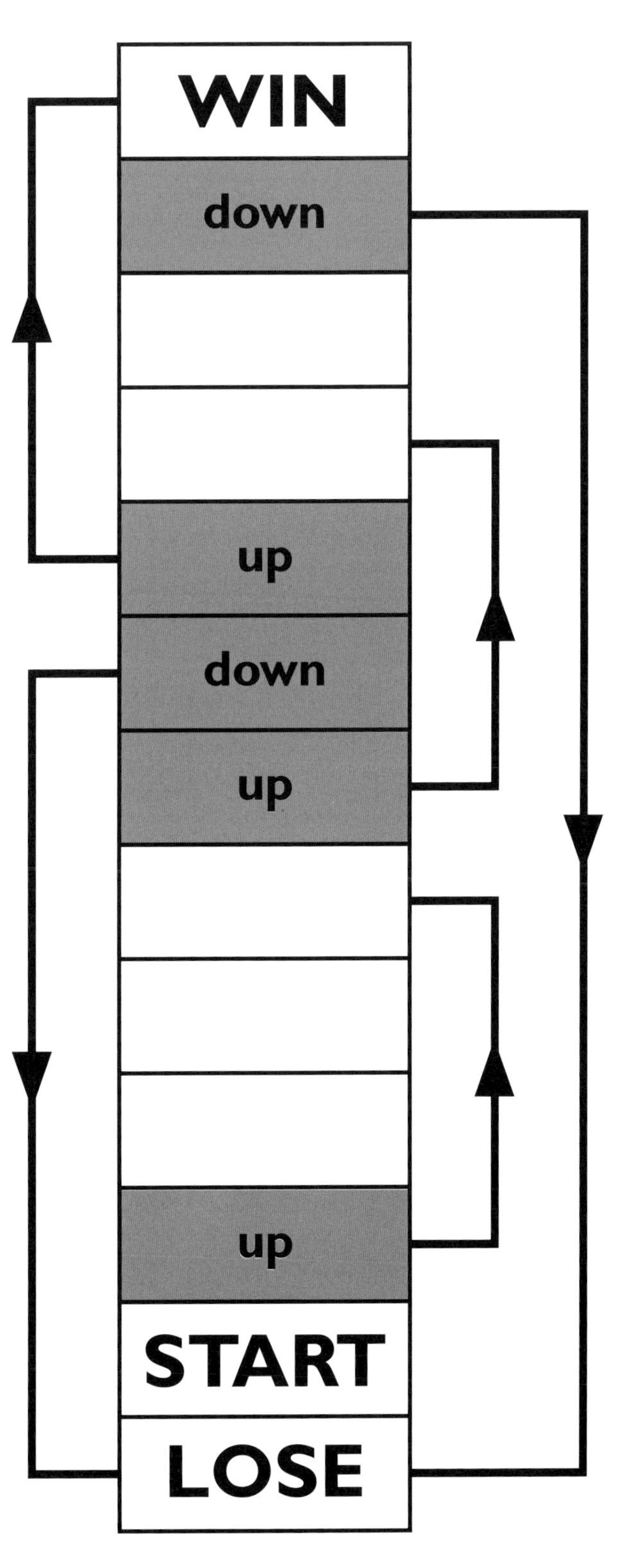

HEXAGON BREAKOUT

Aim:

~To decide whether or not a probability game is fair~

National Curriculum:

~Using and Applying Mathematics 1a, 3a, 3b, 4a; Handling Data 1d, 3a, 3c~

Background:

~Here is another game of chance where you can win or lose, but again you must decide whether or not it is a fair game.~

Homework Activity - Ask the family

Play and talk about this game with someone at home. You are playing together, not against one another.

Instructions

Place a counter on the START.

Roll a normal six-sided dice.

Move ONE SPACE according to the dice score as shown below.

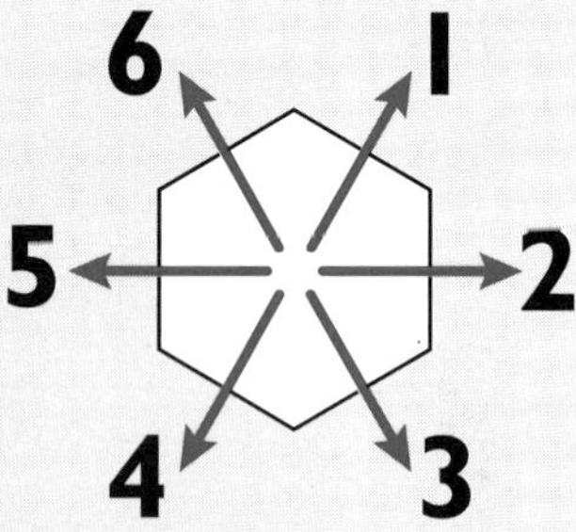

Roll the dice THREE times.

Do you break out into the shaded area after three rolls or do you lose?

Play lots of times and keep a record of the results. Is it a fair game? Give reasons for your answer.

- Suppose it costs 5p to play each time but if you break out you win 10p. Is it worth playing? Give reasons for your answer.
- What if you win 15p for breaking out, or 20p, or 25p, etc?
- What would the winnings have to be for it to be worth playing?

HEXAGON BREAKOUT

EVERYONE'S A WINNER

Aim:

~To decide whether or not a probability game is fair~

National Curriculum:

~Using and Applying Mathematics 1a, 3a, 3b, 4a; Handling Data 1d, 3a, 3c~

Background:

~A game of chance where you win every time, but is it worth playing? Find out for yourself!~

Homework Activity - Ask the family

Play and talk about this game with someone at home. You are playing together, not against one another.

Instructions

Place a counter on the START. Flick two coins (you could flick a coin each).

2 HEADS - move one space north-west.
2 TAILS - move one space north-east.
1 of each - move one space north.
Keep flicking and moving until you WIN.

Play lots of times and keep a record of how much you win. Don't forget to deduct the 20p it costs to play each time. Is it worth playing? Give reasons for your answer.

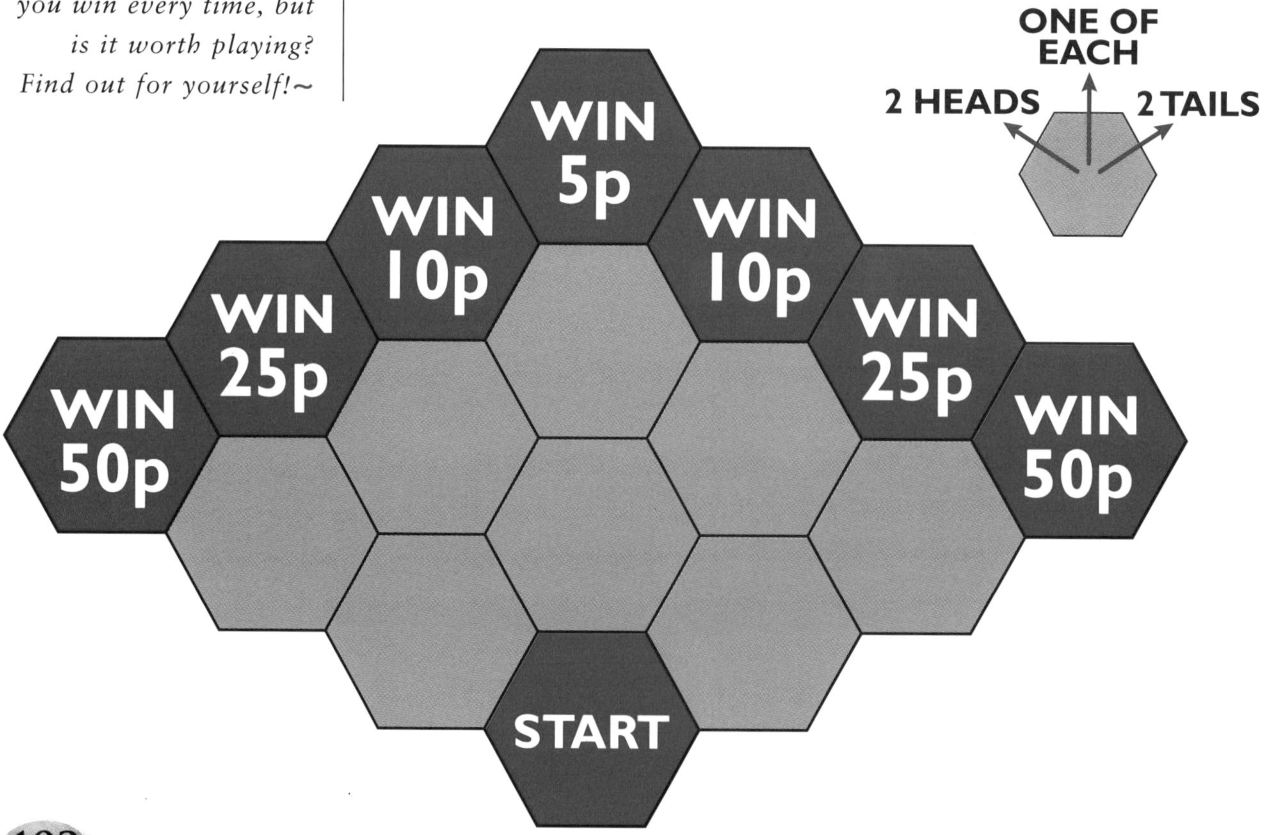

ONE OF EACH
2 HEADS
2 TAILS

WIN 5p
WIN 10p
WIN 10p
WIN 25p
WIN 25p
WIN 50p
WIN 50p
START

STICK, TWIST OR PIG

Homework Activity - Ask the family

Players take it in turn to roll a six-sided dice. You score points according to the roll of the dice, i.e. roll a 4 and you score 4 points. After your first roll you can 'twist' and immediately have another roll to score more points. You can 'twist' as many times as you like and keep adding to your score. **BUT** if at any time you roll a 6 you lose all of your points for that turn (shout 'pig') and the dice passes to the next player for their turn. At any time during your turn you can 'stick' and so keep the points you have scored on that turn. These points are added to your grand total. The dice then passes to the next player.

Before playing the game you might like to investigate a few things.

Roll a dice lots of times (at least 100) and keep a record of the scores. What is the maximum number of rolls before getting a six? What is the minimum number? What is the average number? What are the maximum, minimum and average scores before getting a six? Make a note of this information and bring it in to school.

Use this information to help you make decisions whilst playing the game.

Explain in your own words how you used the information.

Aims:

~To play a probability game~

~To understand the nature of random events~

National Curriculum:

~Using and Applying Mathematics 1a, 2a, 4a; Handling Data 1b, 1d, 2d, 3a~

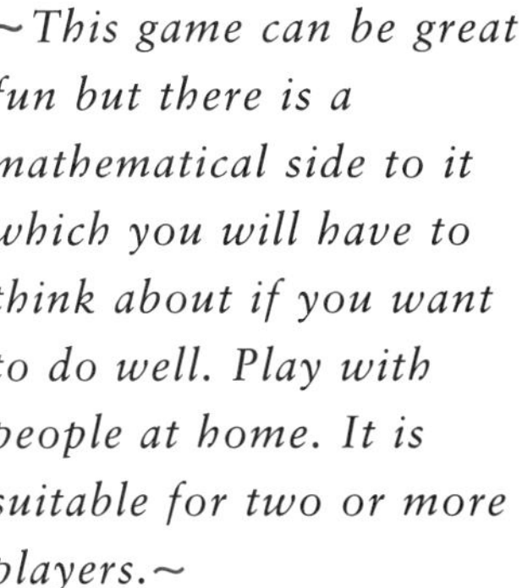

Background:

~This game can be great fun but there is a mathematical side to it which you will have to think about if you want to do well. Play with people at home. It is suitable for two or more players.~

WHO CHEATED?

Aims:

~To carry out a simple probability experiment~

~To understand the nature of random events~

National Curriculum:

~Using and Applying Mathematics 1a, 2a, 4a; Handling Data 1d, 3a~

Background:

~Have you ever cheated when doing your homework? Of course not! In this activity you have to spot the cheat but you must give reasons for your decision, and it should be based on an understanding of how random events can turn out.~

Homework Activity

A teacher asked her class to do a probability experiment for homework. The pupils were asked to flick a coin fifty times and make a note of the results.

Here are one pupil's results.

H T T H H T H T H T T H T T H H T H H T H H T T H

T T H T H T H H T H T H H T T H T T H T H H T T H

Here are another pupil's results.

H T T T H H T T H H H H T T H T H T T T H H T T T

T H T H H H H T T H T T H T T T H T H T T T H T T

One of these pupils actually did the experiment and one of them made up the results.

Can you tell which one is which?

Give reasons for your answer.

~ Ask the family ~

Working with someone at home, flick a coin fifty times and make a note of the results. One of you can flick while the other writes.

Compare your results with the two sets of results above. This might help you to decide who cheated. What does the other person think? Can they spot the odd one out? Ask them to give reasons for their answer and make a note of them.

WIN THE POOLS

Homework Activity - Ask the family

Most newspapers predict the following Saturday's football results by putting a 1, 2 or X for each match:

1 if they think the home team will win

2 if they think the away team will win

X if they think it will be a draw.

Get hold of a copy of the predictions in a newspaper. When the matches have been played, check the predictions against the actual results. How good were they? Work out some figures that show how good the predictions were.

Use a six-sided dice to predict the results. Roll the dice for each match.

If the dice score is 1 or 2 then the prediction is a home win.

If the dice score is 3 or 4 then the prediction is an away win.

If the dice score is 5 or 6 then the prediction is a draw.

Check the dice predictions against the actual results. How good were the dice predictions? Work out some figures that show how good they were. Were they better or worse than the predictions in the newspaper? Give reasons for your answer and show any figures you work out.

Do you think the allocation of the dice score to the three possible results (i.e. 1 or 2 is Home, 3 or 4 is Away, 5 or 6 is Draw) is a good one? Can you think of a better way of using the dice scores? Can you think of an alternative to using a dice? Give reasons for your answers.

Aim:

~To investigate ways of predicting football results~

National Curriculum:

~Using and Applying Mathematics 1a, 2a, 4a; Number 1b; Handling Data 1b, 1d, 3a~

Background:

~Winning a raffle or lottery is all down to chance, but what about the football pools? Is it down to skill in predicting the results or just good fortune? In this activity you must investigate how good the football pools experts are at predicting results. Work on this activity with someone at home.~

MASTER SHEETS FOR PHOTOCOPYING

Do not draw or write on the following pages.
They can be photocopied and used in some of the activities in this book.

Glossary of Mathematical Words used in this Book

area
An amount of covering or the amount of space a flat shape takes up. Area is measured in square units such as square centimetres (cm^2) and square metres (m^2).

capacity
The amount of 3-D space inside a container or the quantity of liquid a container will hold. Capacity is measured in millilitres (ml) and litres (l). Also see *volume*.

congruent
If two shapes are congruent then they are exactly the same. One shape could be cut out and fitted exactly on top of the other.

cube
A 3-D shape with six faces which are all squares.

If you *cube* a number then you multiply it by itself twice, e.g. 5 cubed (5^3) is 5 x 5 x 5 = 125. Also see *cube root*.

cube root
The number which when multiplied by itself twice gives you the required answer e.g. the *cube root* of 125 is 5. Also see *cube*.

cuboid
A 3-D shape with six faces which are all rectangles.

factors
The *factors* of 15 are 1, 3, 5 and 15, i.e. the numbers which will divide into 15.

line of symmetry
A line which divides a flat shape into two identical halves. These would map onto one another if the shape was folded along the line of symmetry.

multiples
The multiples of 7 are 7, 14, 21, 28, 35, ...

net
A flat shape which could be cut out and folded together to form a 3-D shape.

palindrome
A number, word or sentence which is the same when the digits or letters are reversed, e.g. RADAR and 71817.

pentomino
A flat shape made out of five connected squares.

perimeter
The distance around the outside of a flat shape.

plane of symmetry
The 3-D equivalent of a *line of symmetry*. A straight cut which divides a 3-D shape into two identical halves which map onto one another either side of the cut.

polygon
A flat shape whose sides are all straight lines, e.g. a square, a triangle, a hexagon etc.

prime numbers
A number which has no *factors* apart from the number itself and 1, i.e. it can only be divided by itself and 1.

rotational symmetry
A shape has rotational symmetry if it can be turned through a quarter-turn, half-turn or other fraction of a turn and still look exactly the same as it did in its original position.

similar
Two shapes are similar if one is an enlargement of the other, e.g. all snooker tables should be similar because the length is always twice the width, regardless of the actual dimensions.

square numbers
If you *square* a number then you multiply it by itself, e.g. 8 squared (8^2) is $8 \times 8 = 64$. Also see *square root*.

The *square numbers* are 1, 4, 9, 16, 25, 36, 49, 64, ...

square root
The number which when multiplied by itself gives you the required answer, e.g. the *square root* of 81 is 9. Also see *square numbers*.

surface area
The total area of all the faces of a 3-D shape. Surface area is measured in the same units as area. Also see *area*.

tessellation
An arrangement formed by fitting together many copies of the same flat shape with no gaps between them.

volume
The amount of solid matter in a 3-D shape or, in the case of a hollow shape, the amount of 3-D space inside. Volume is measured in cubic units such as cubic centimetres (cm^3) and cubic metres (m^3). Also see *capacity*.

Your Notes

Your Notes

Your Notes

Your Notes

Your Notes

Your Notes

Your Notes

Your Notes